# This Book Belongs to:

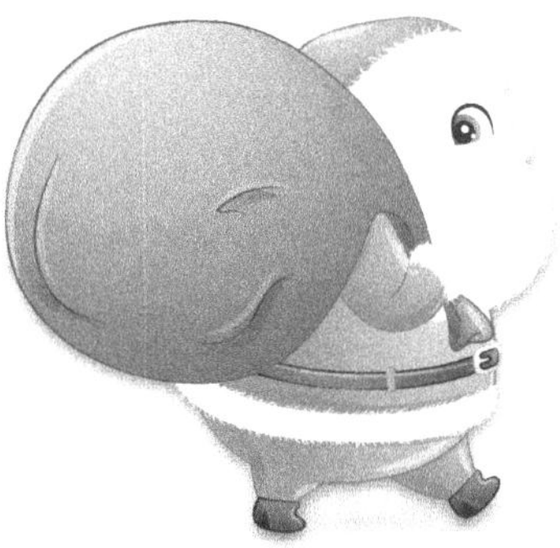

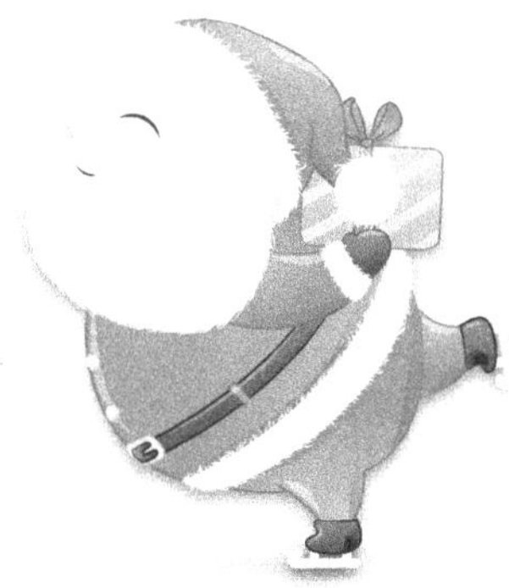

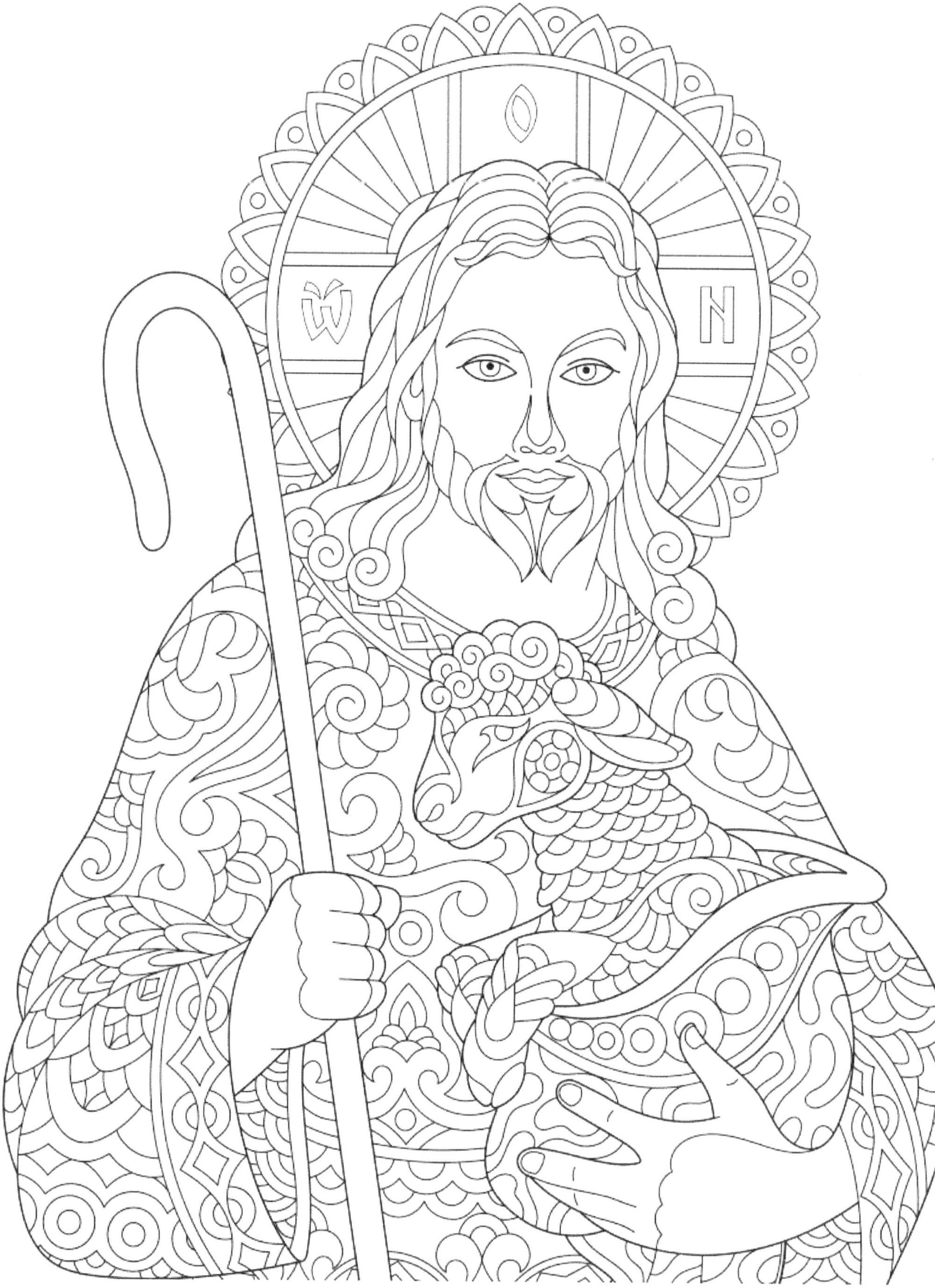

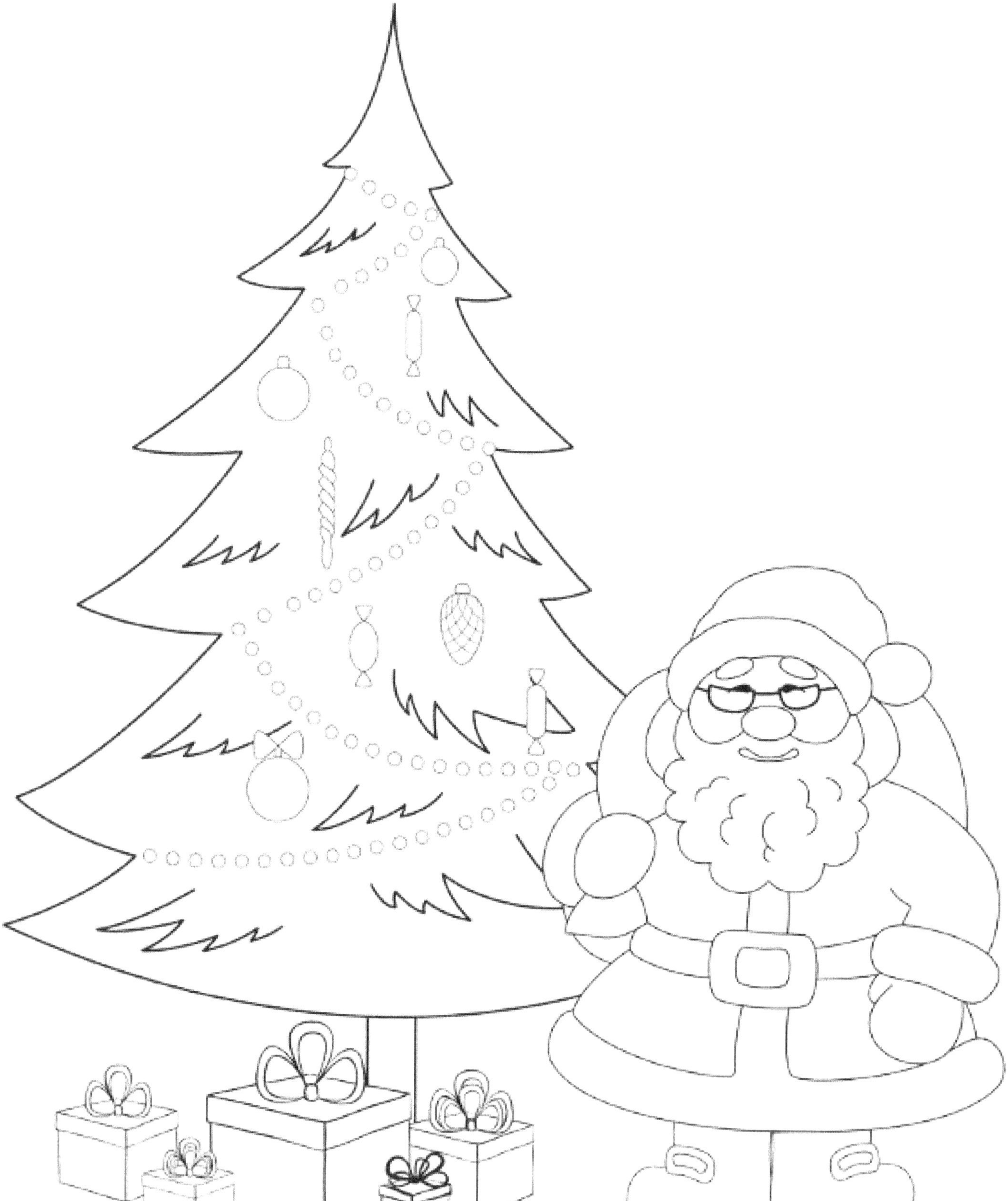

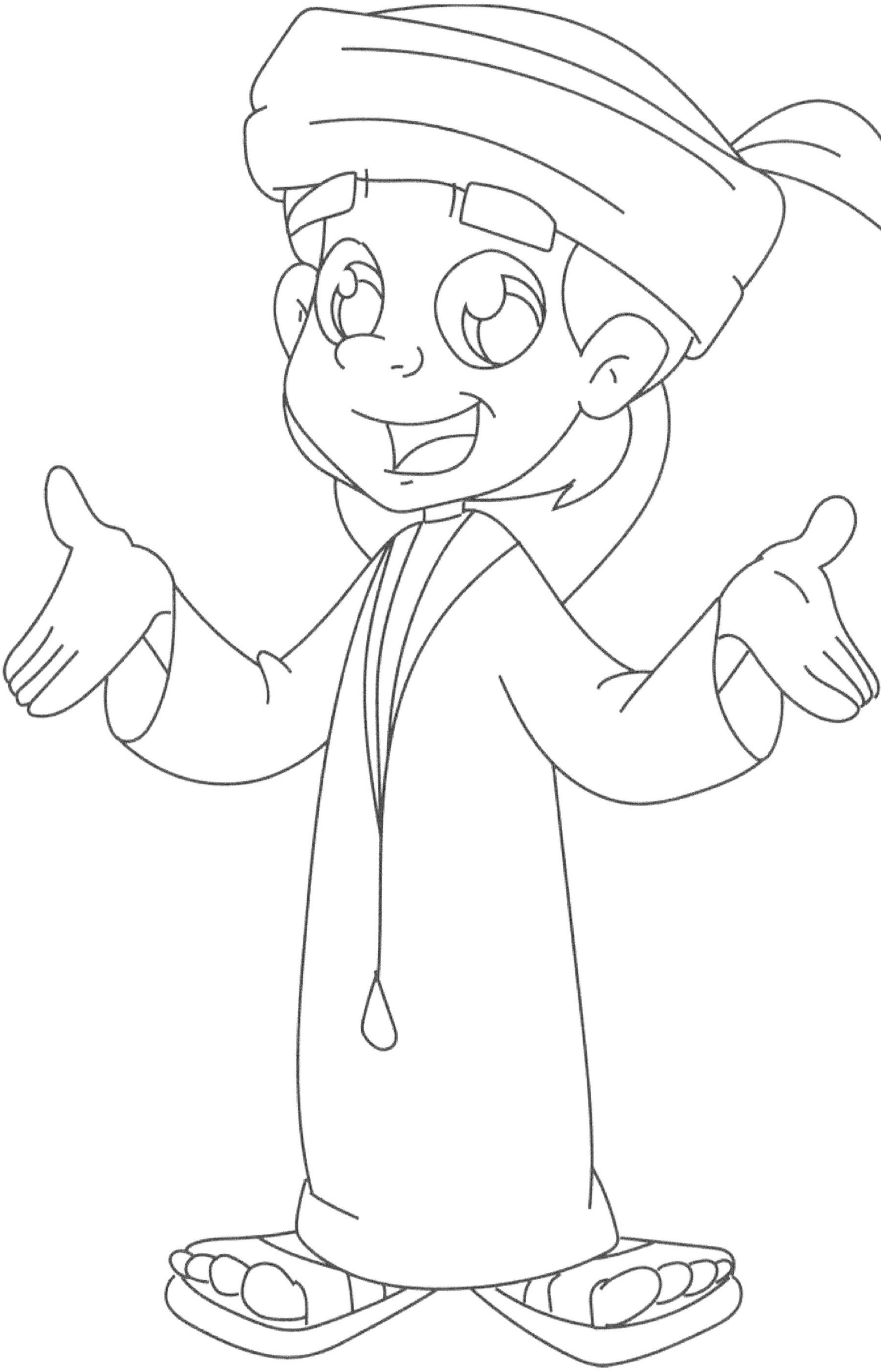

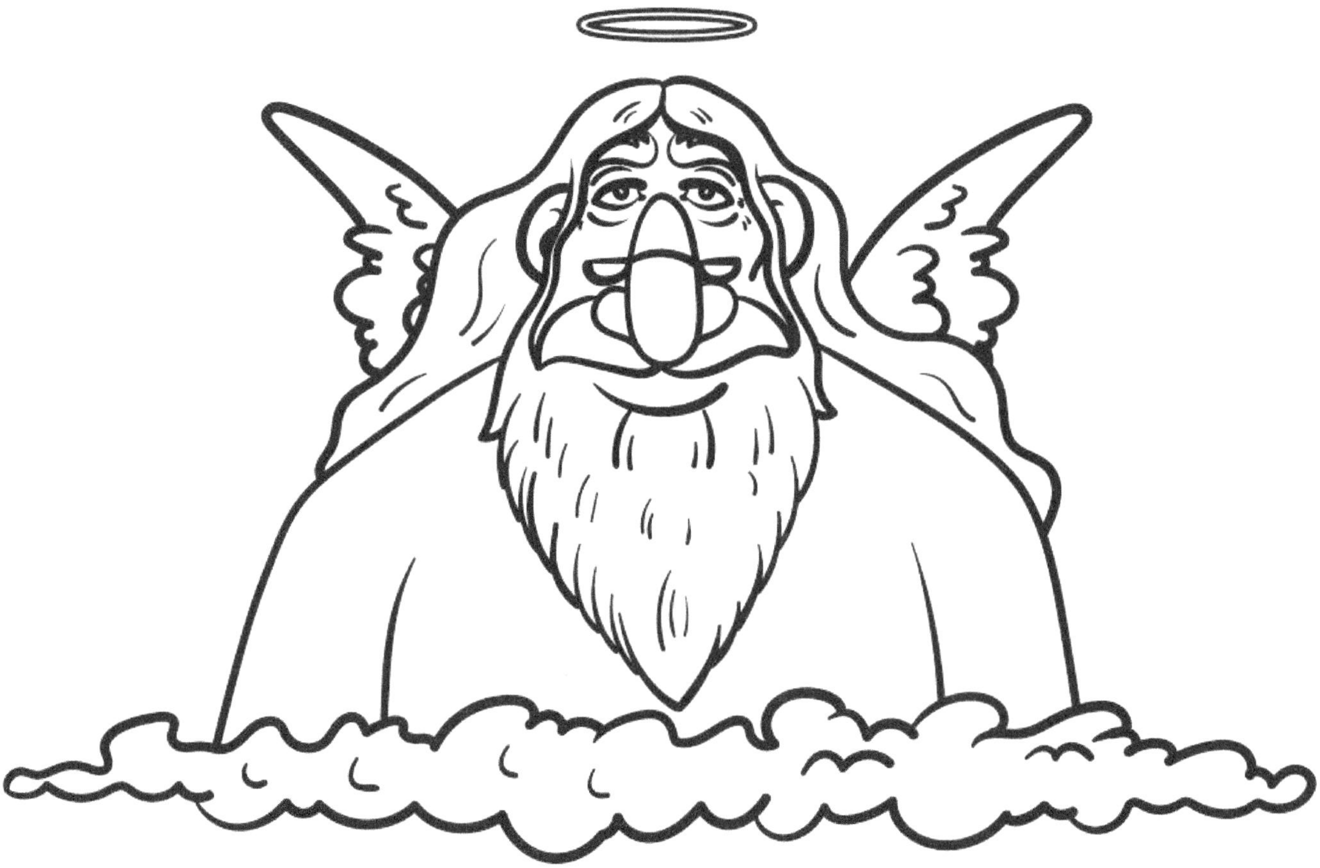

# אמא של שבת

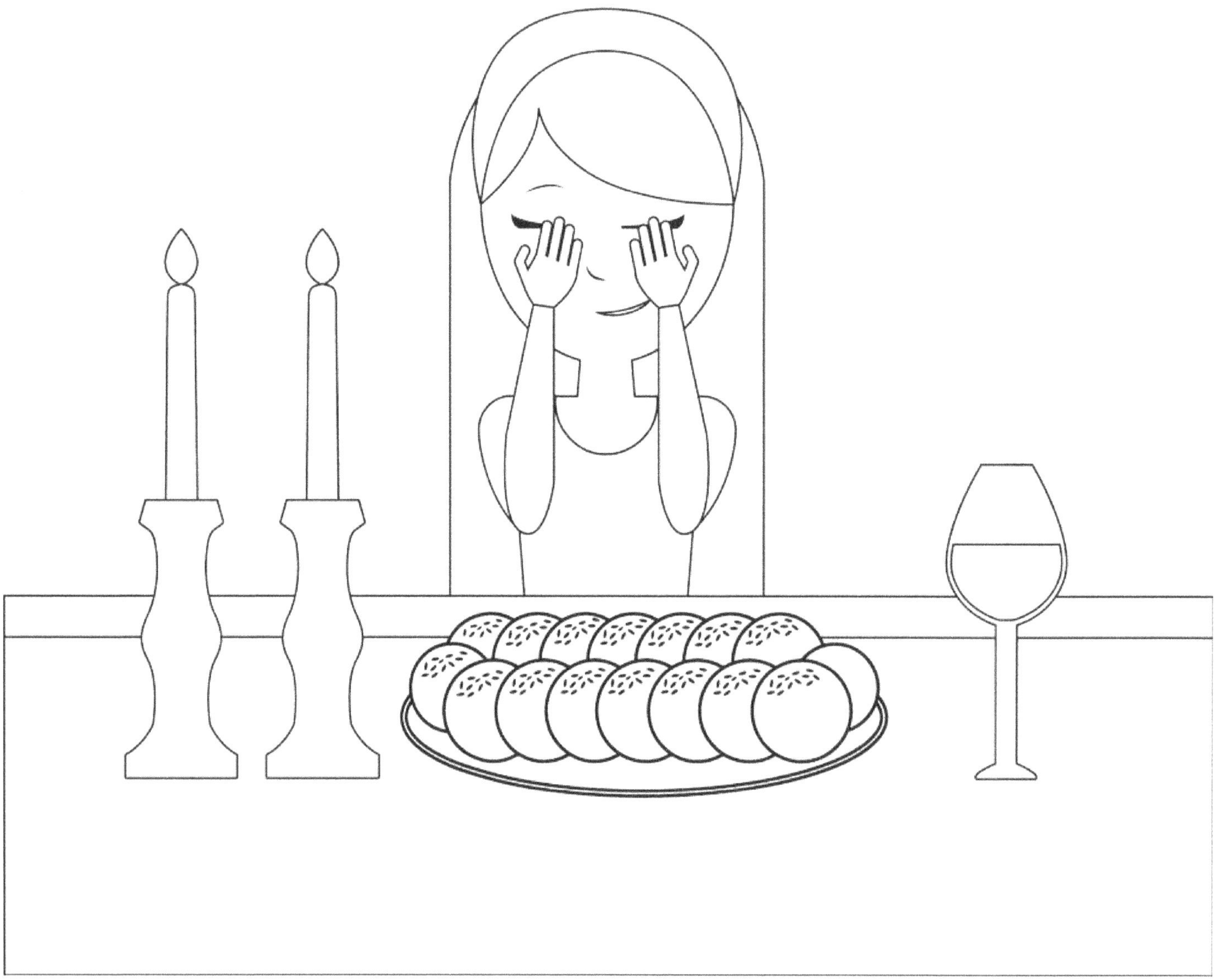

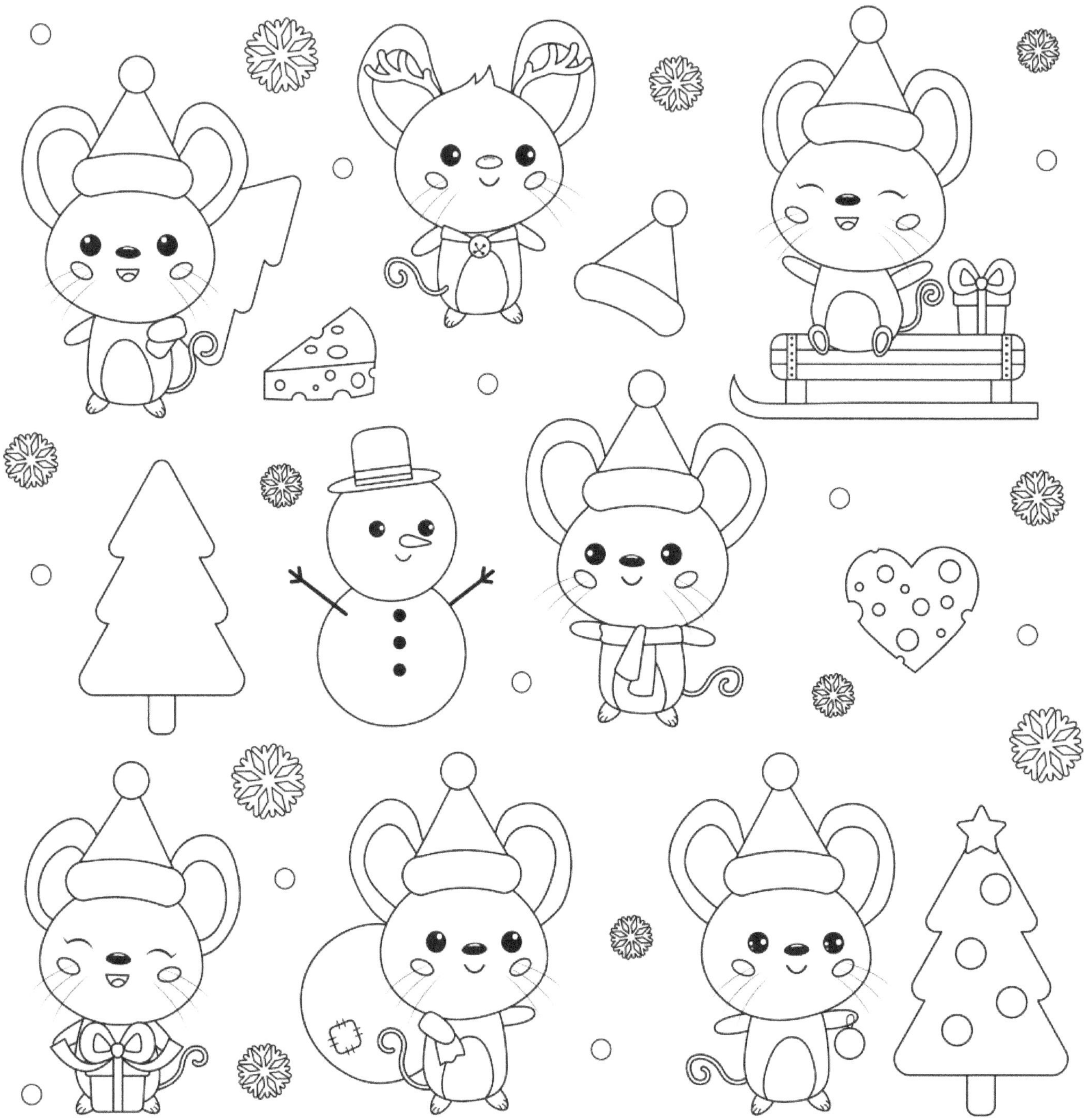

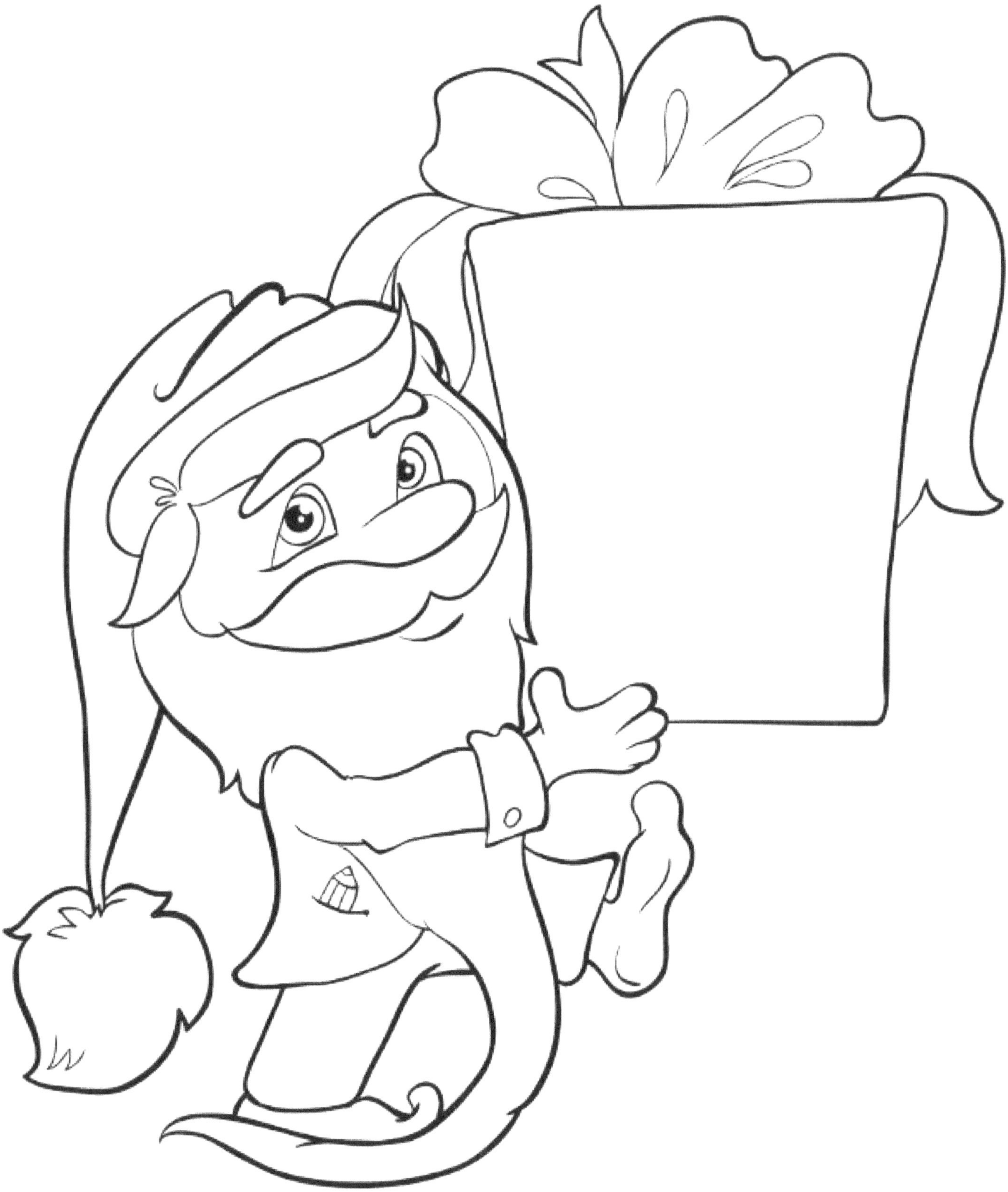

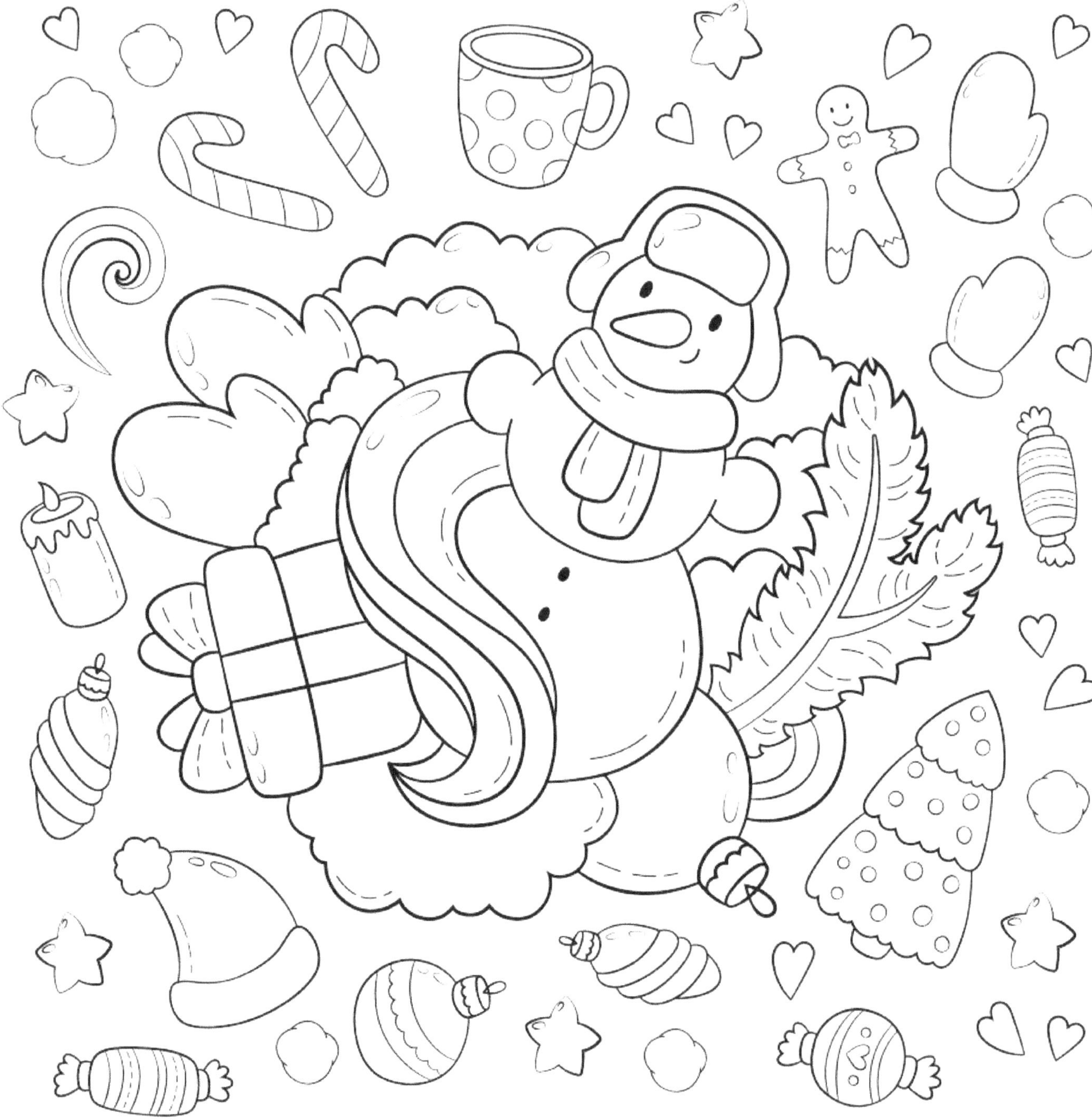

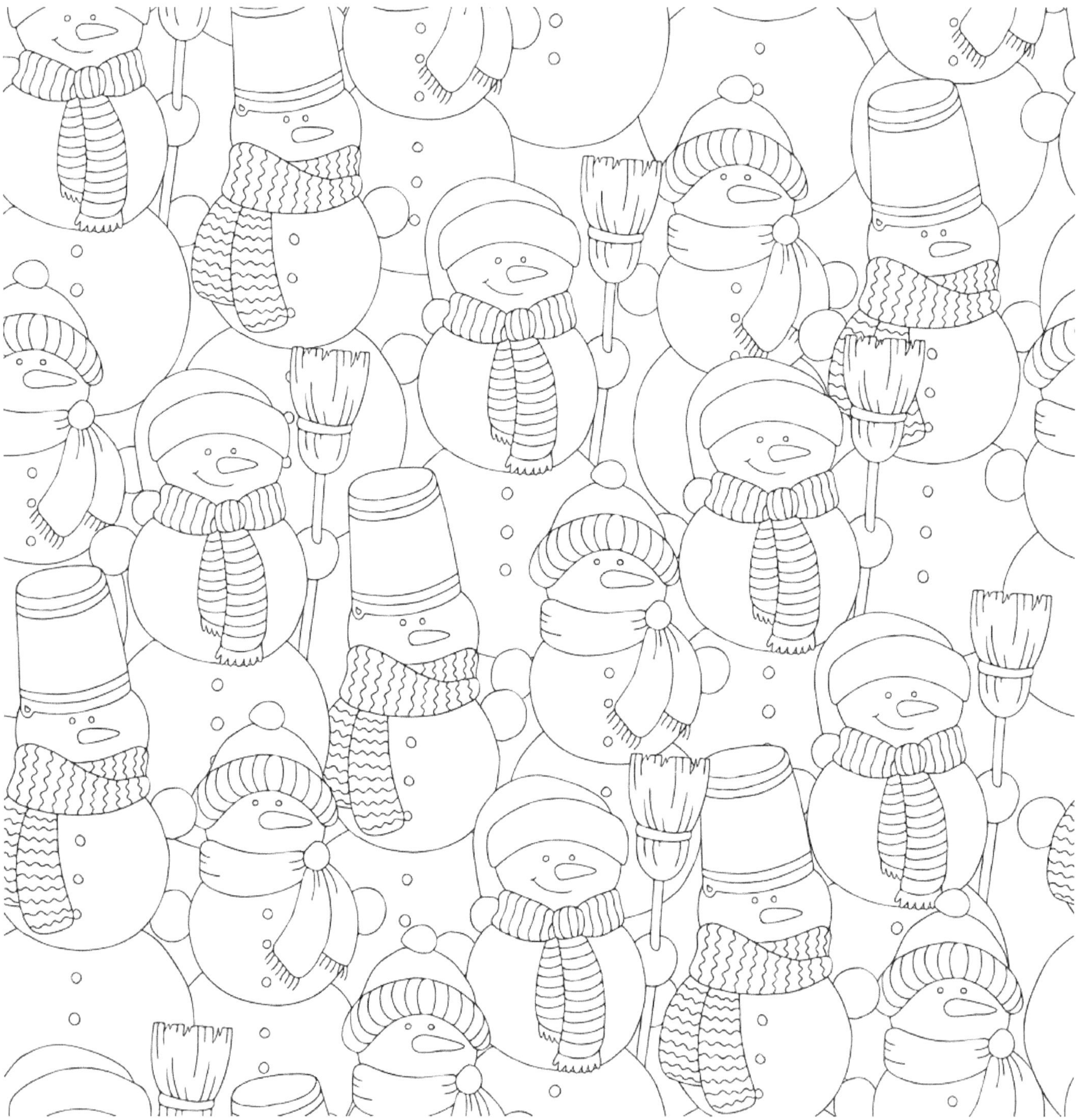

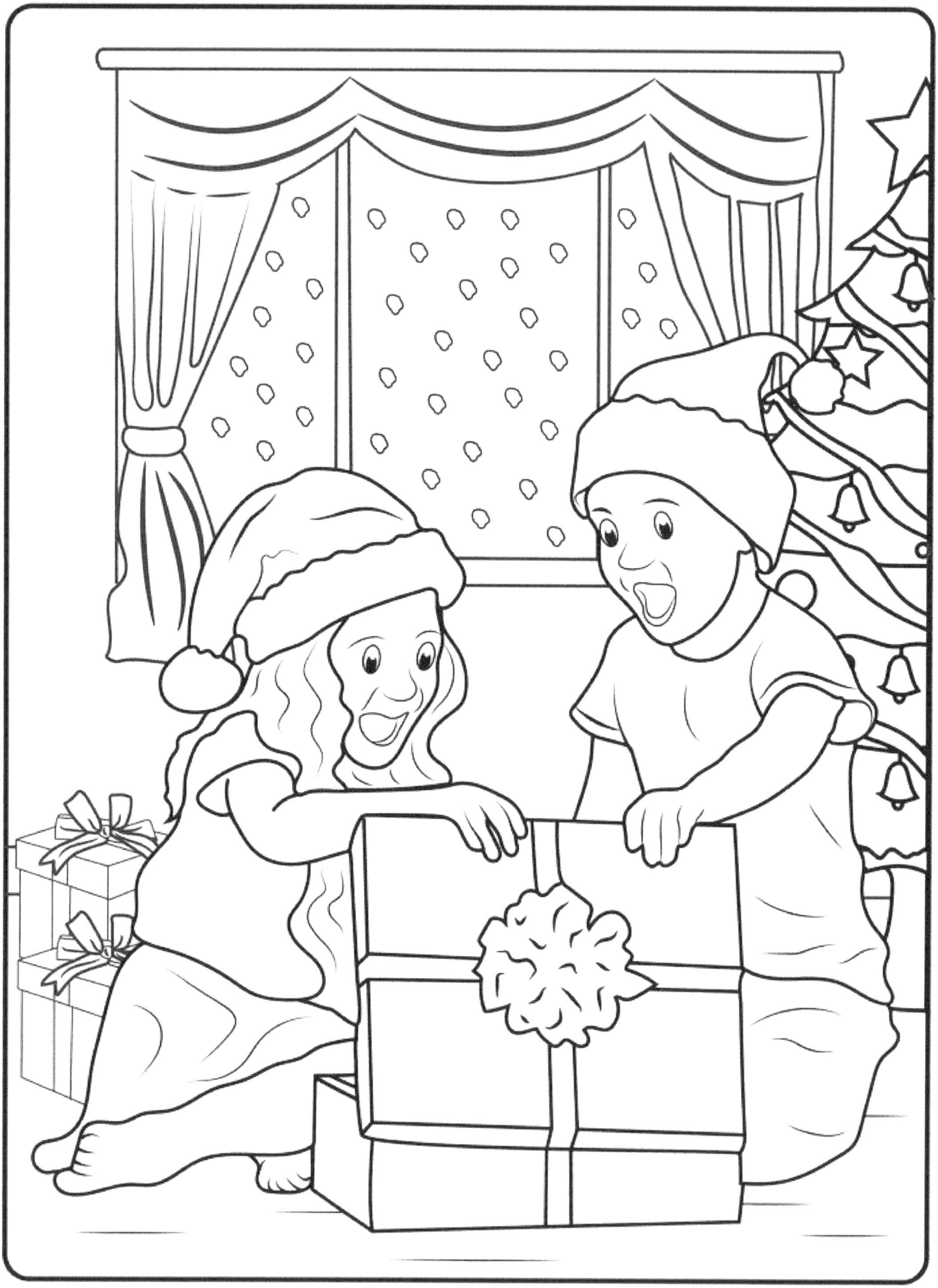

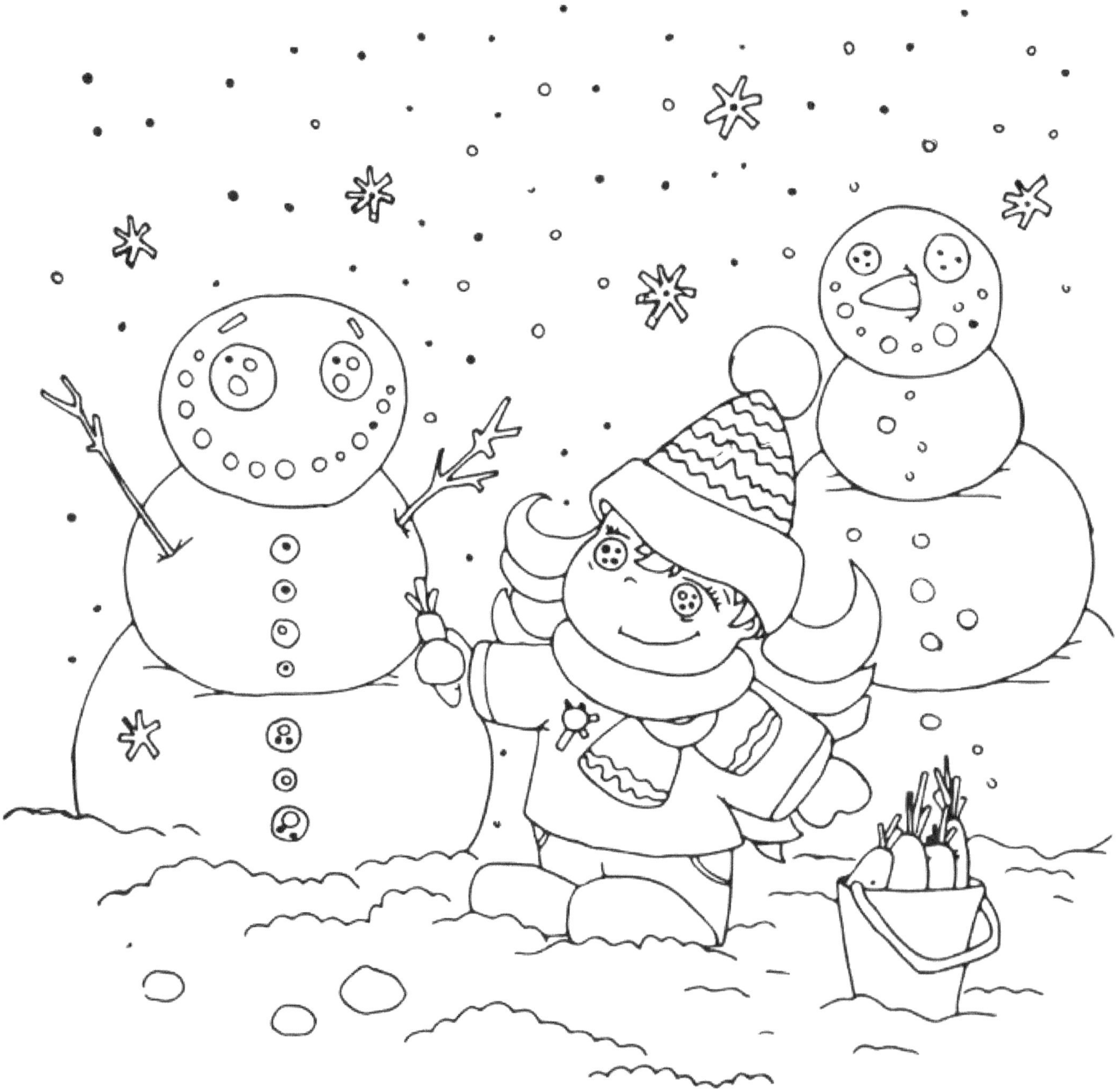

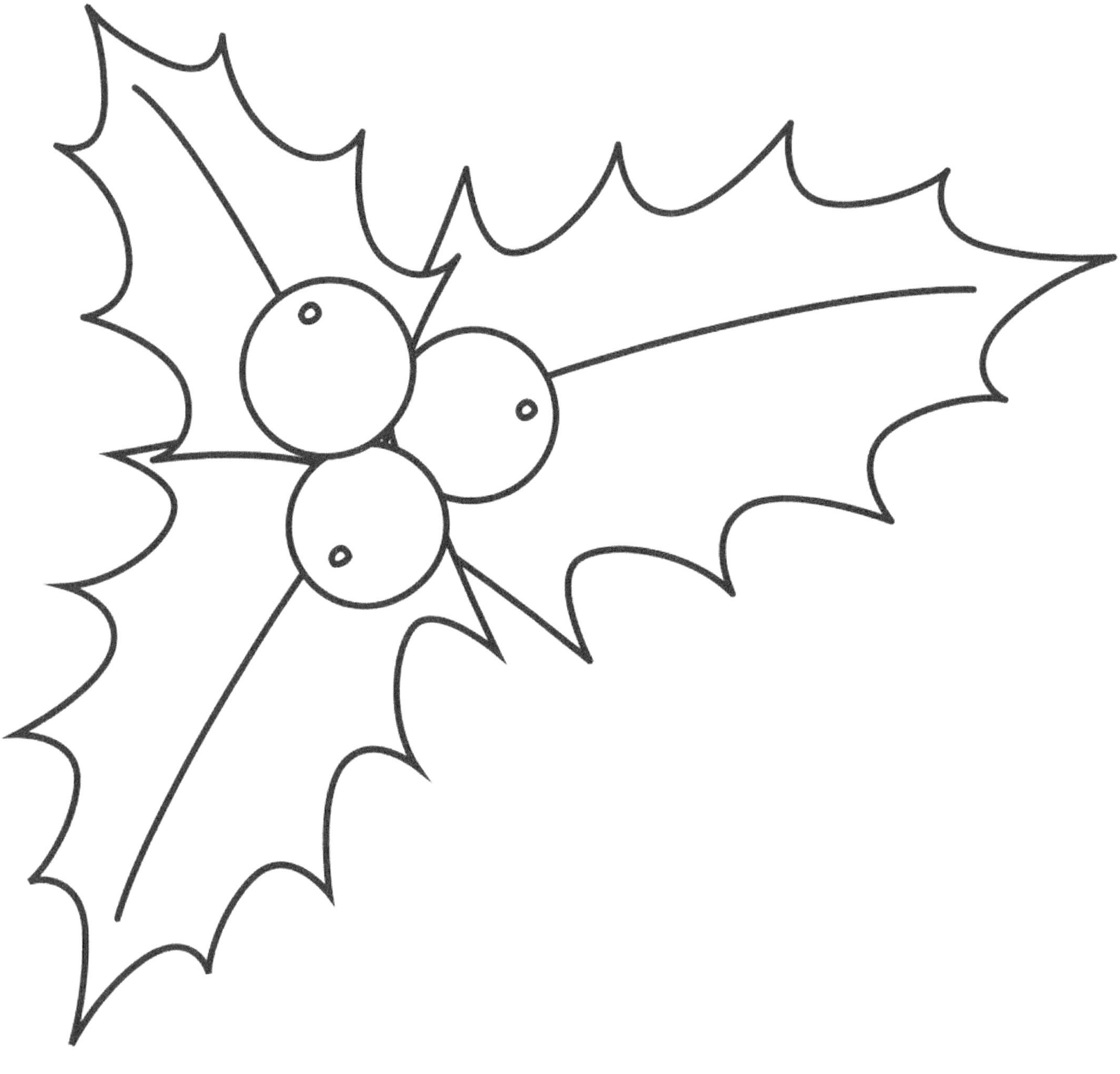

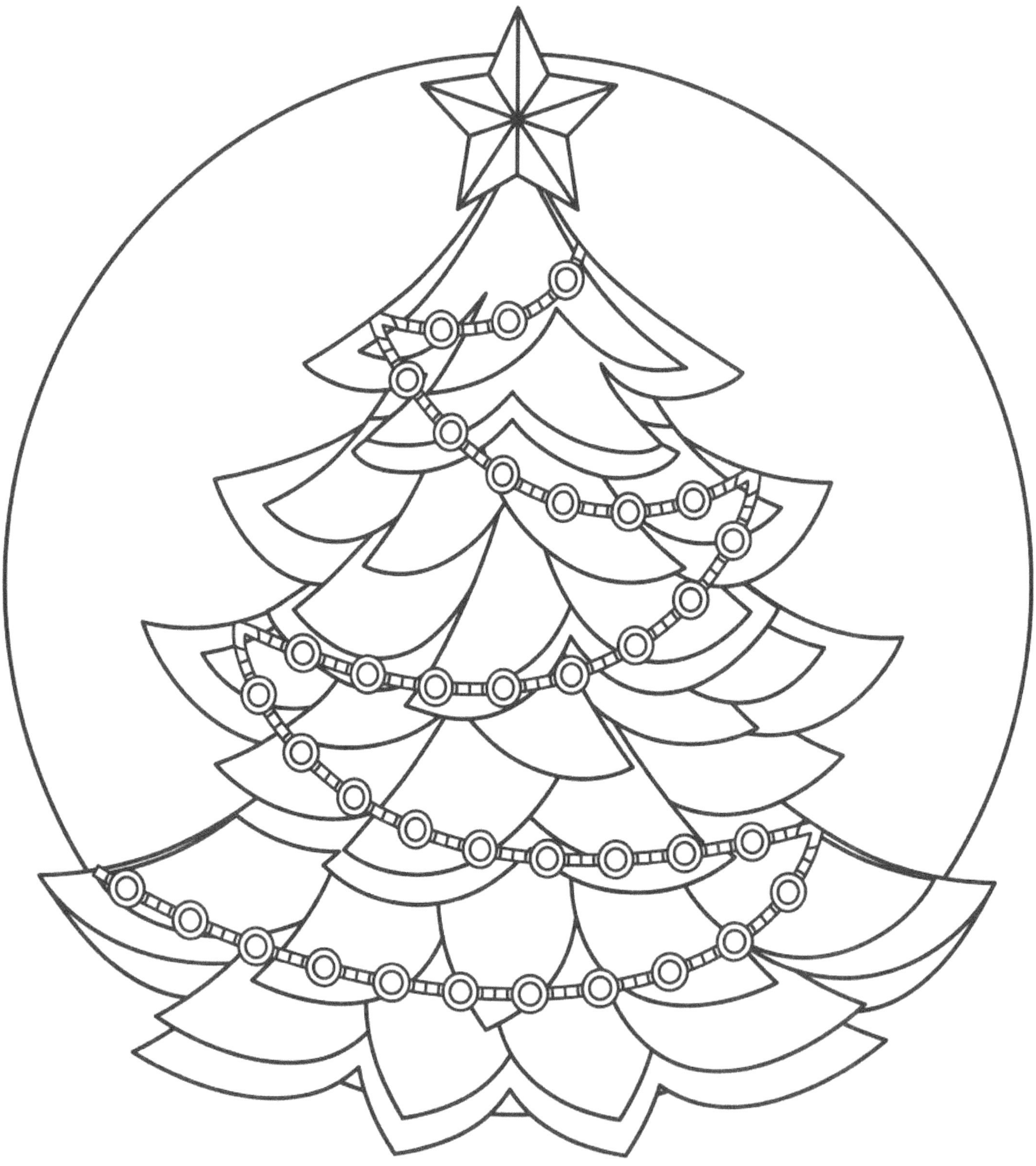

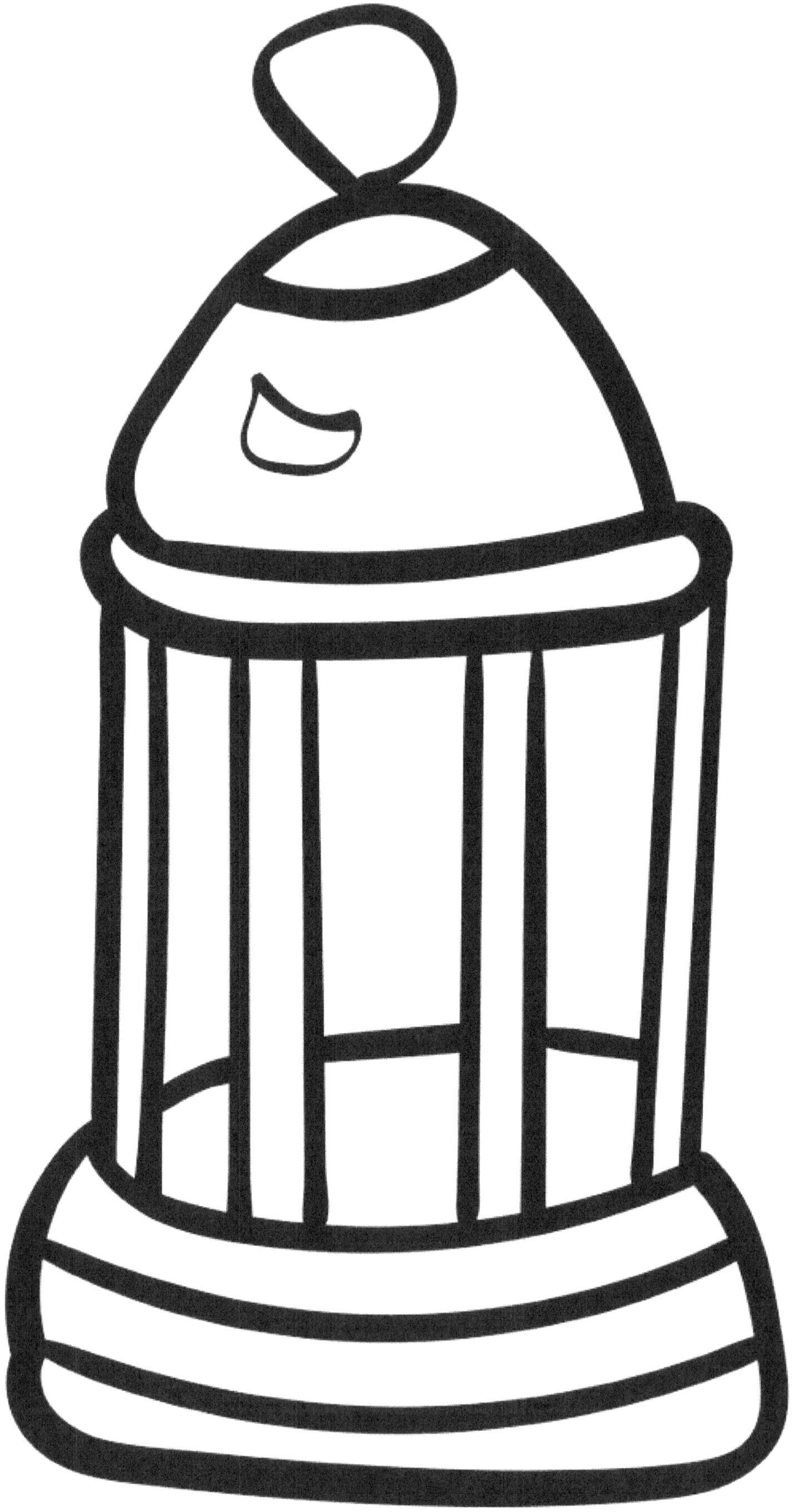

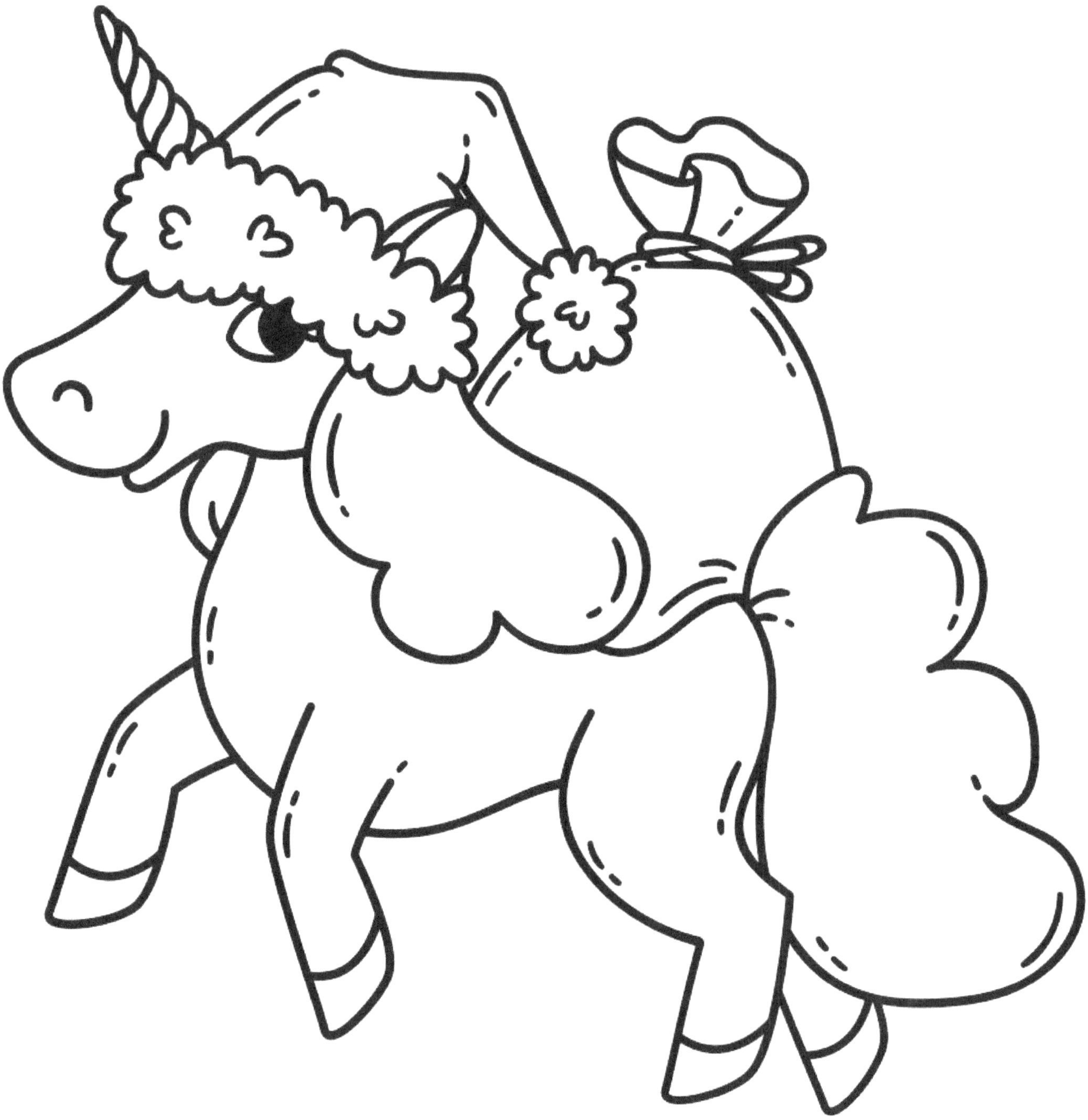

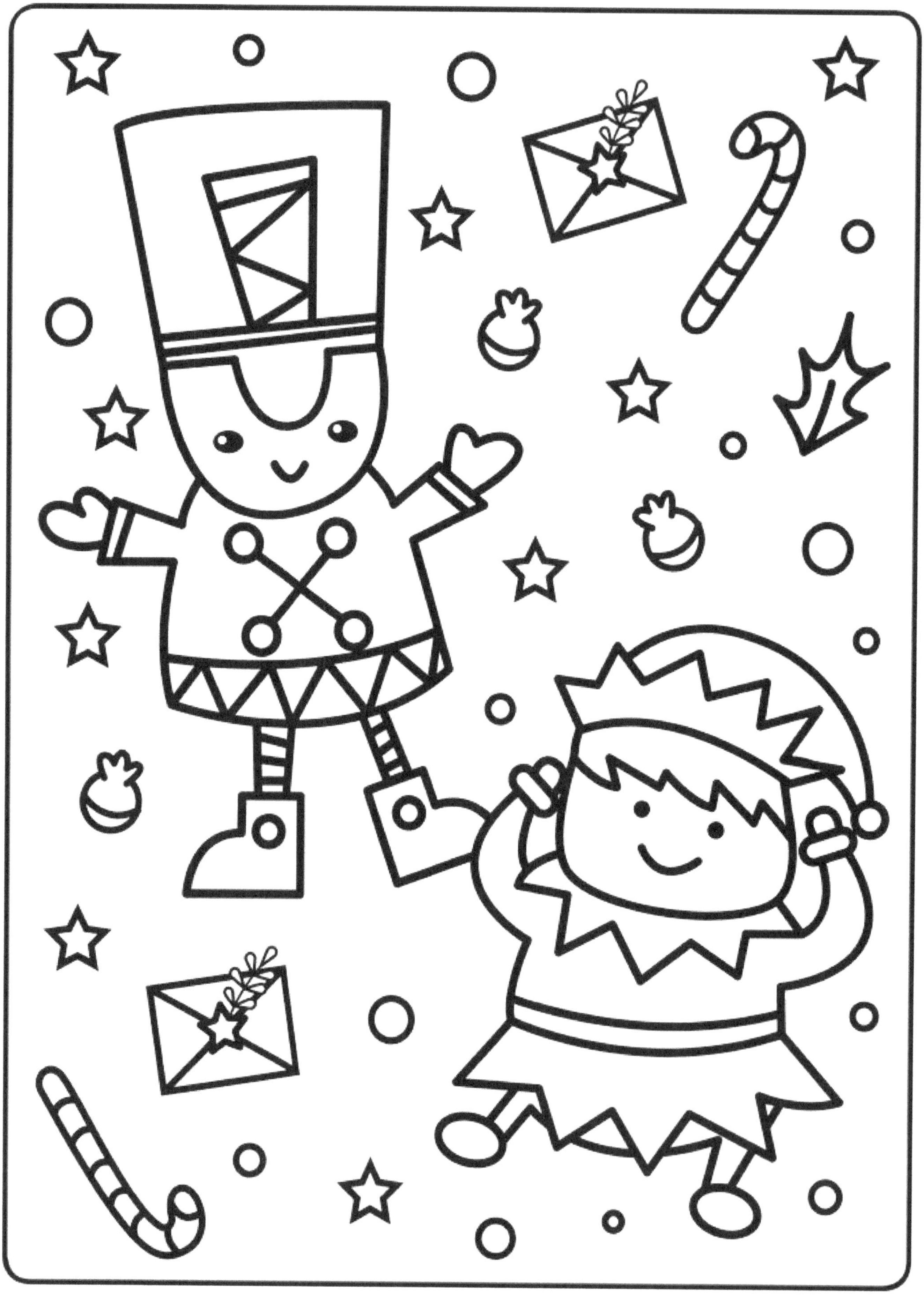

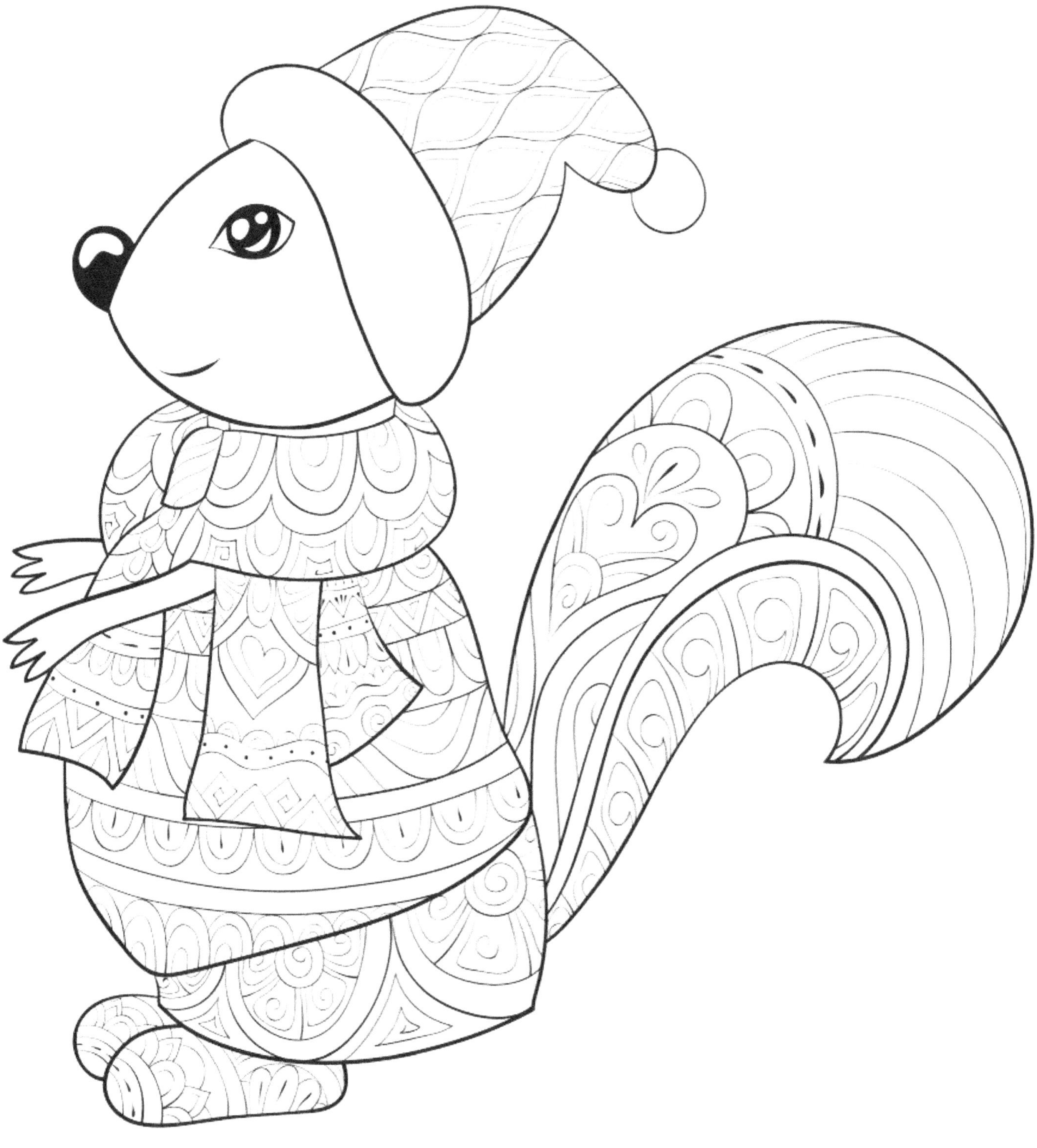

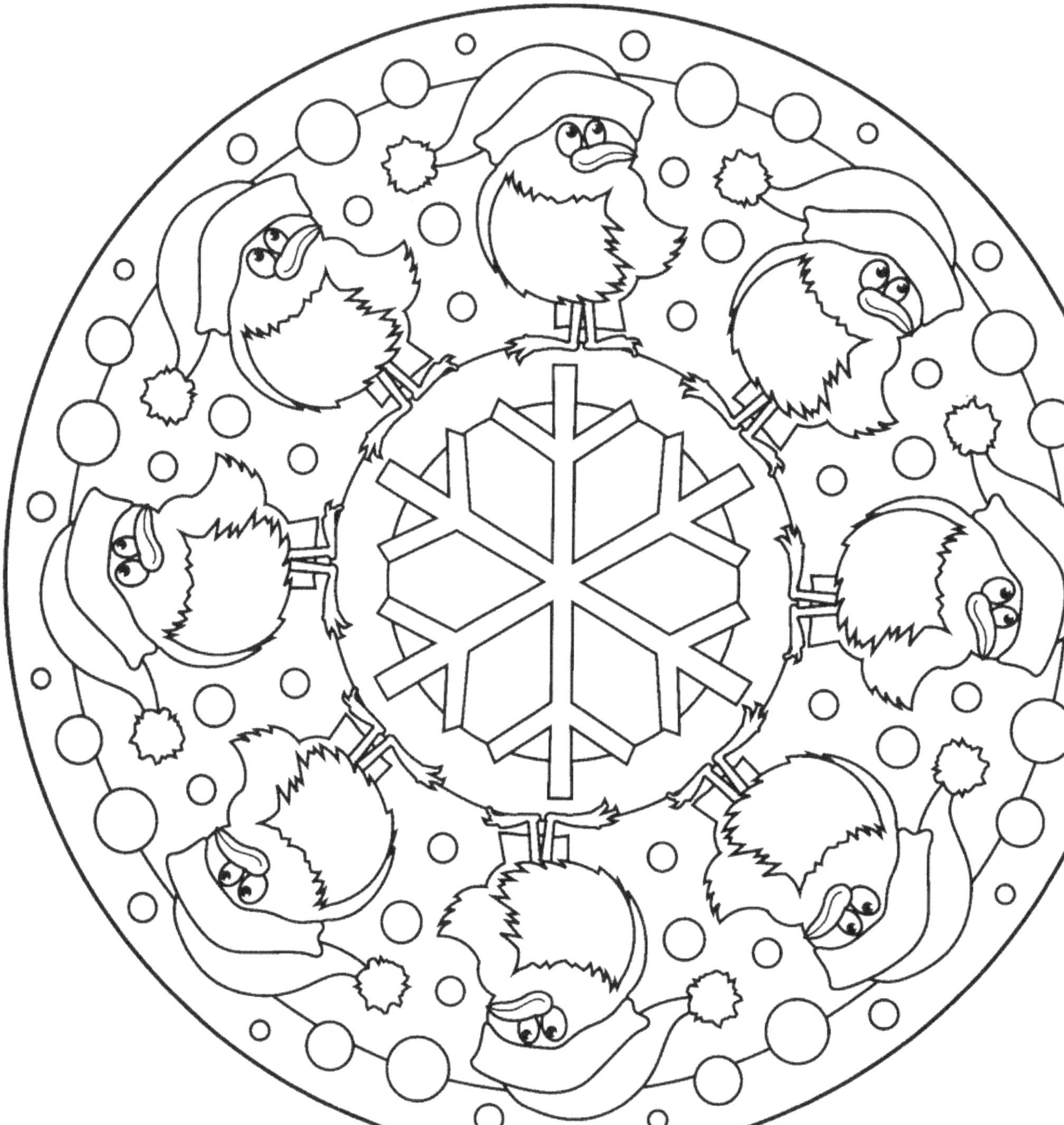

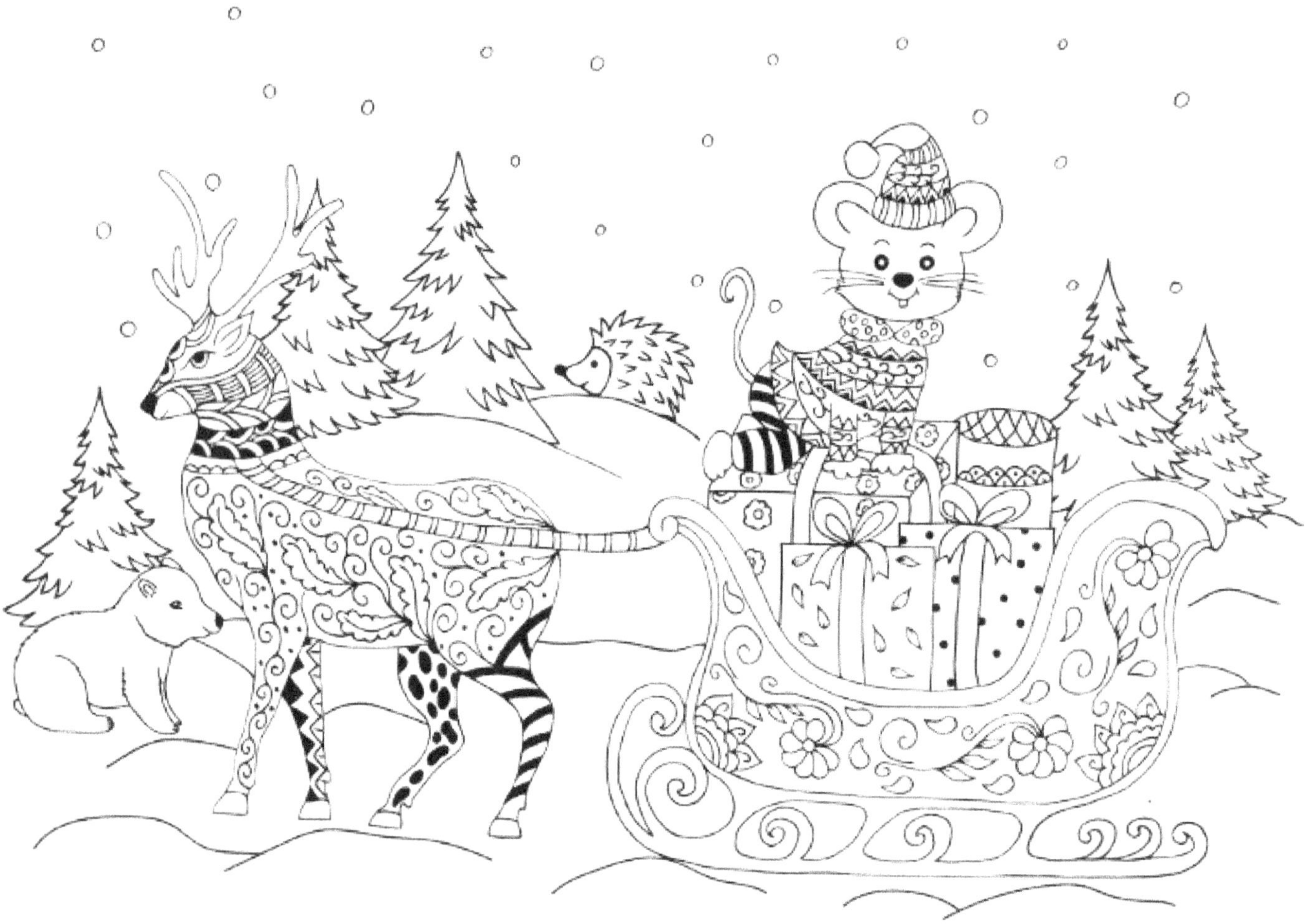

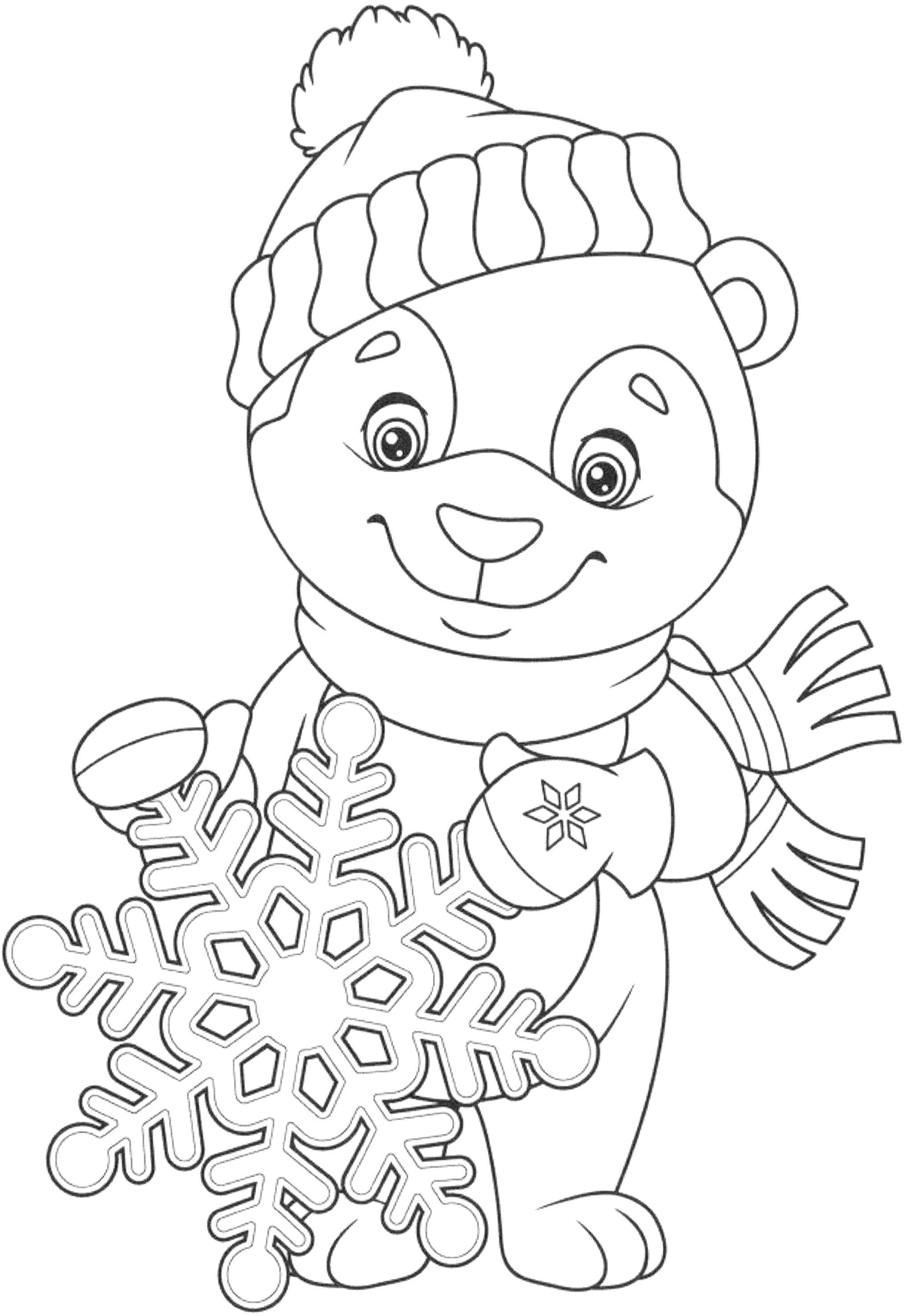

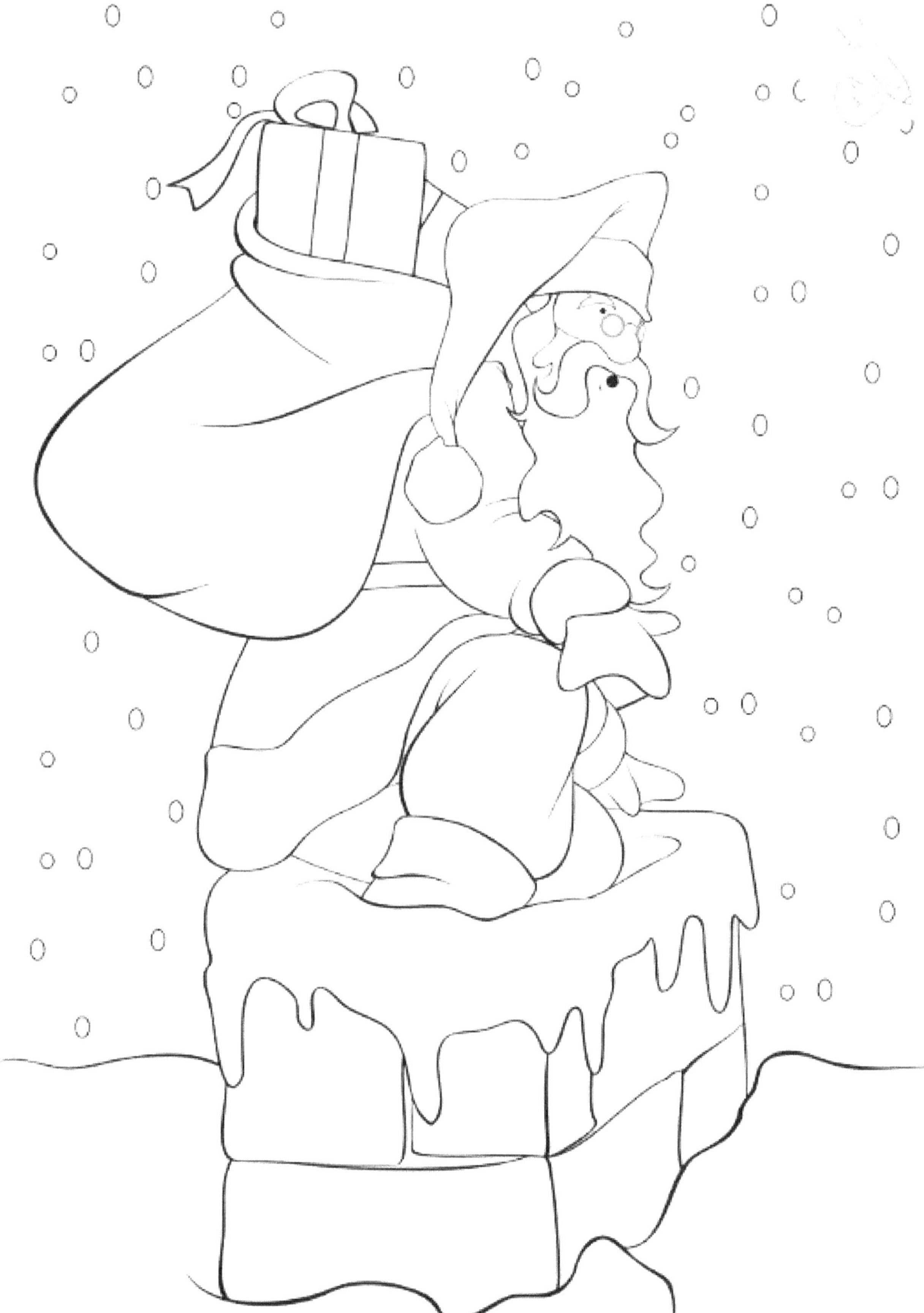

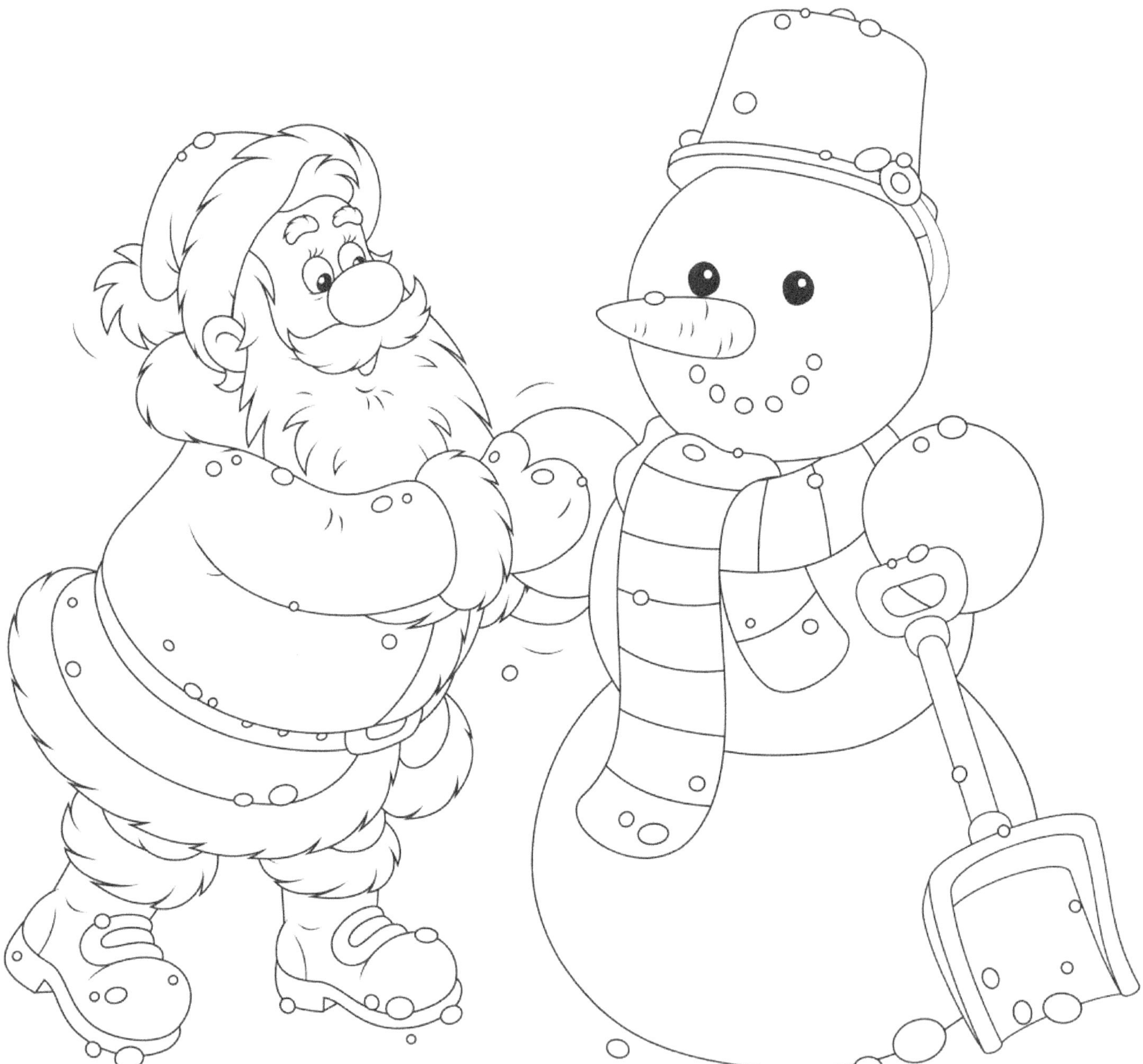

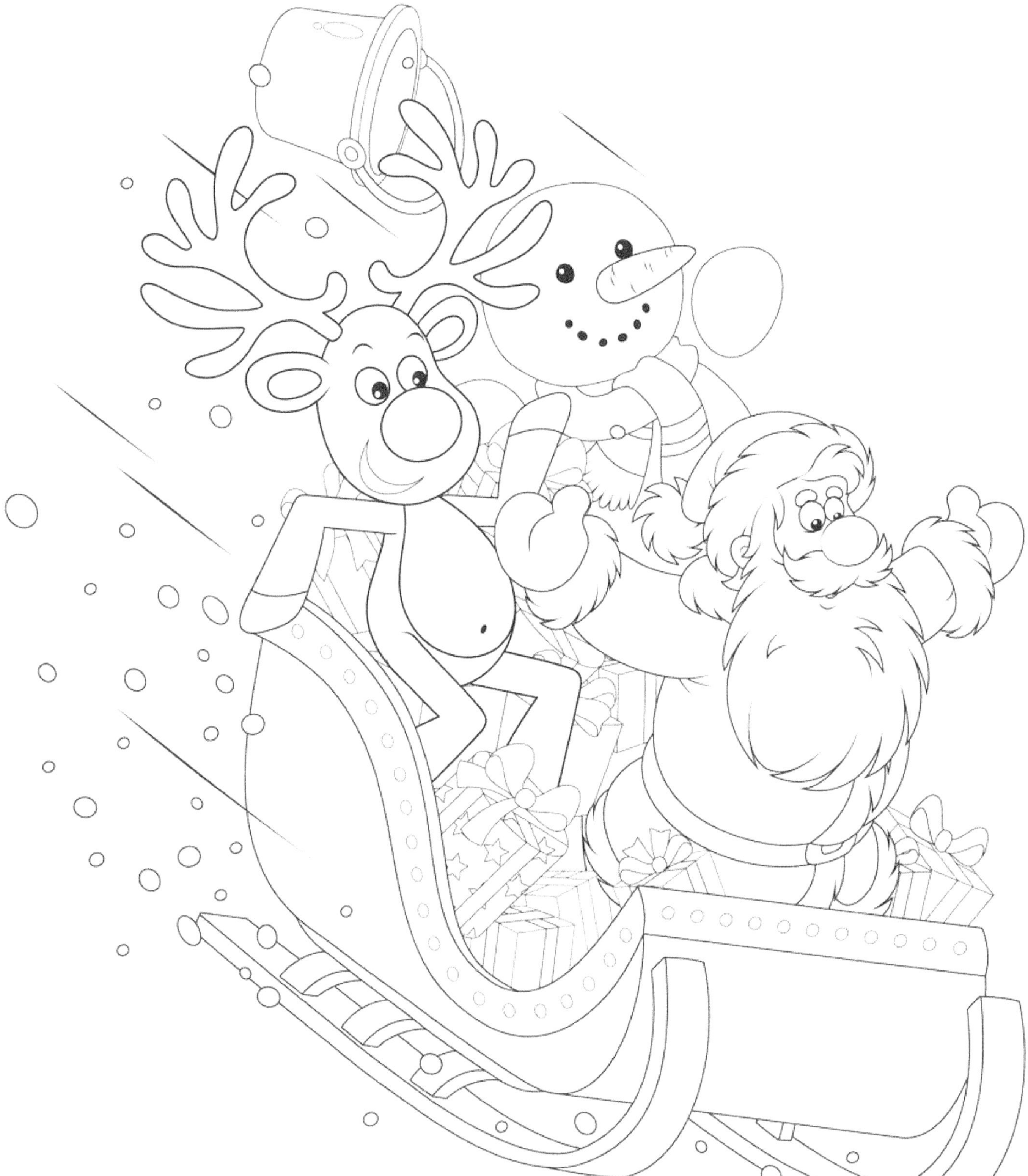

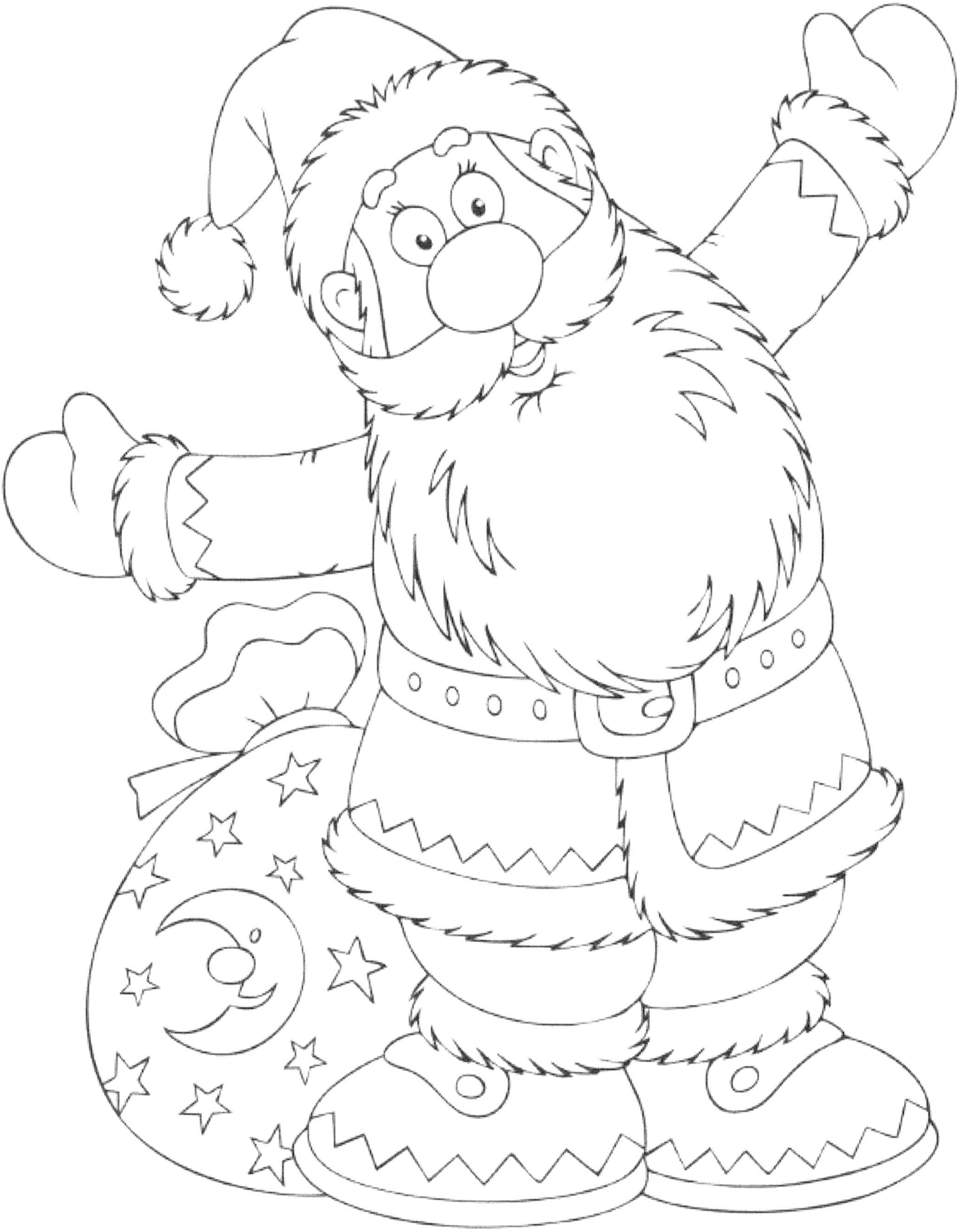

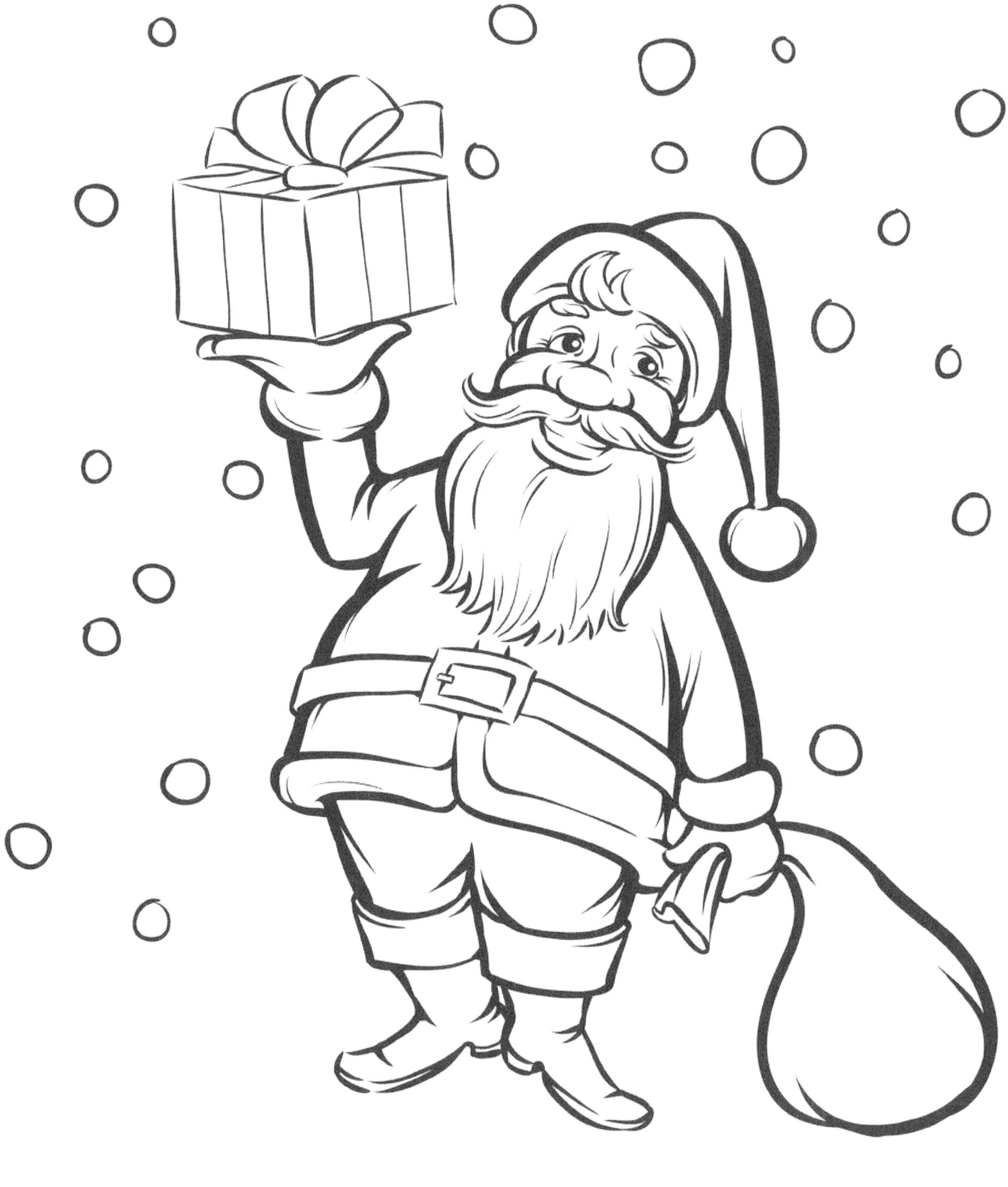

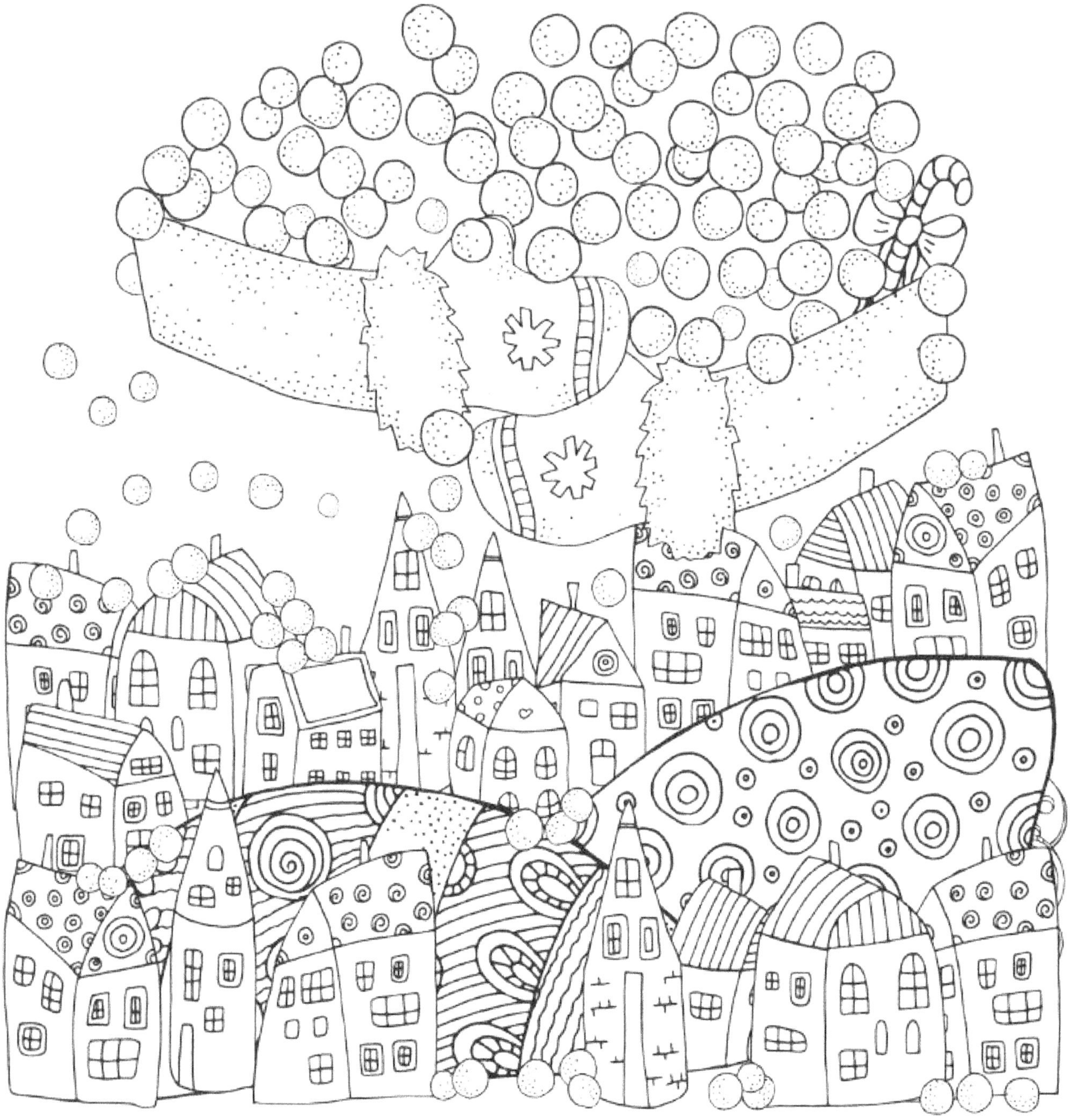

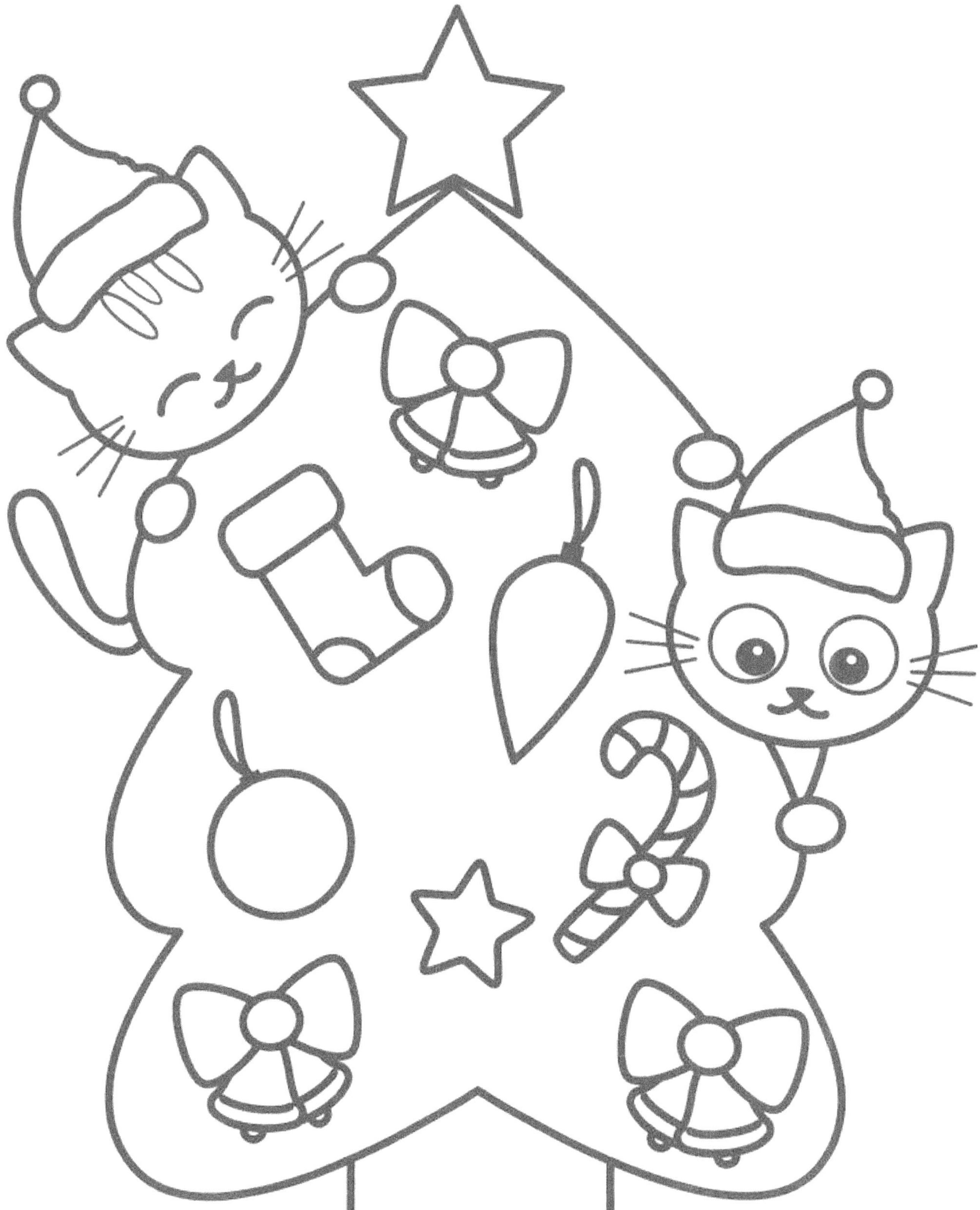

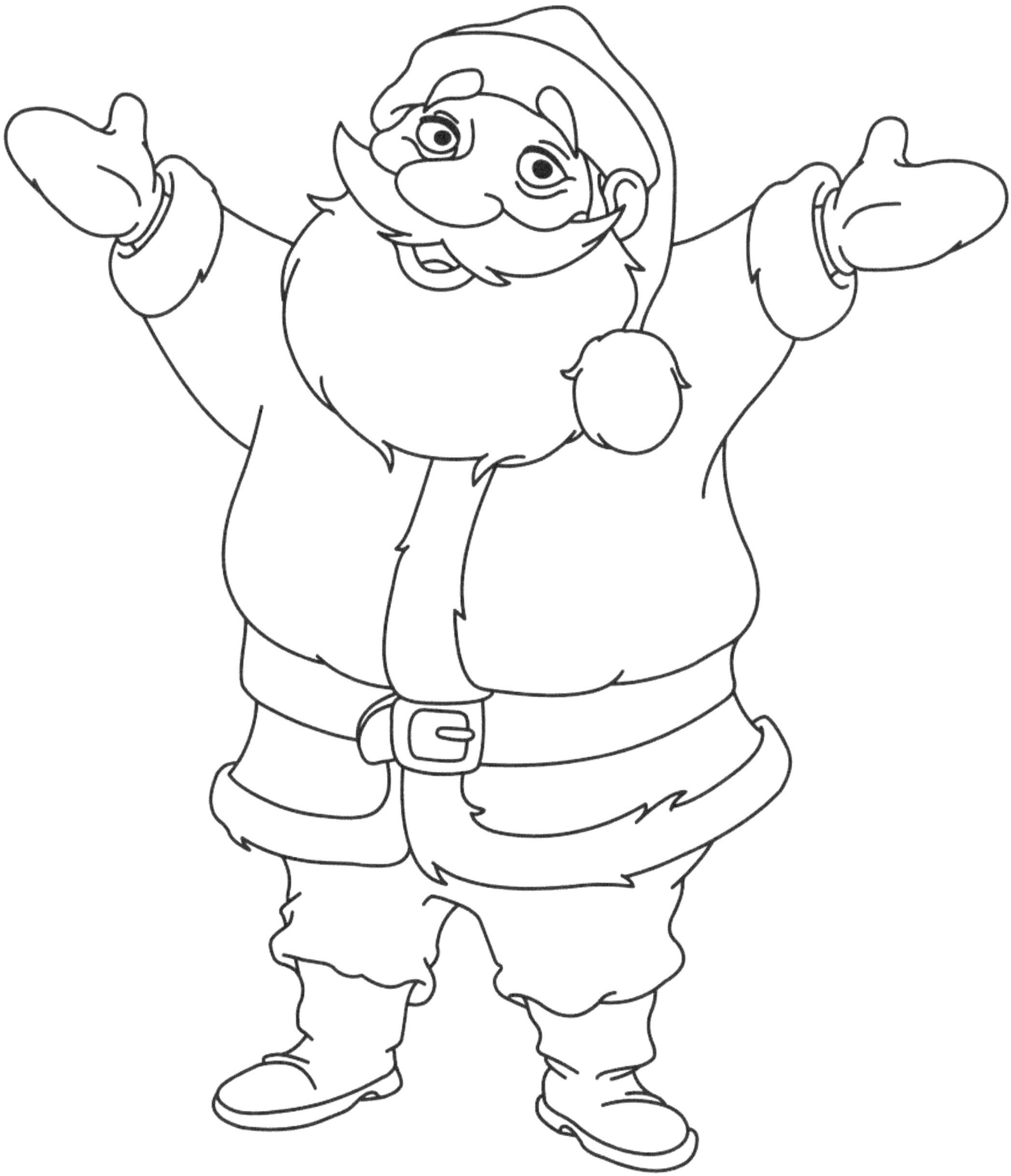

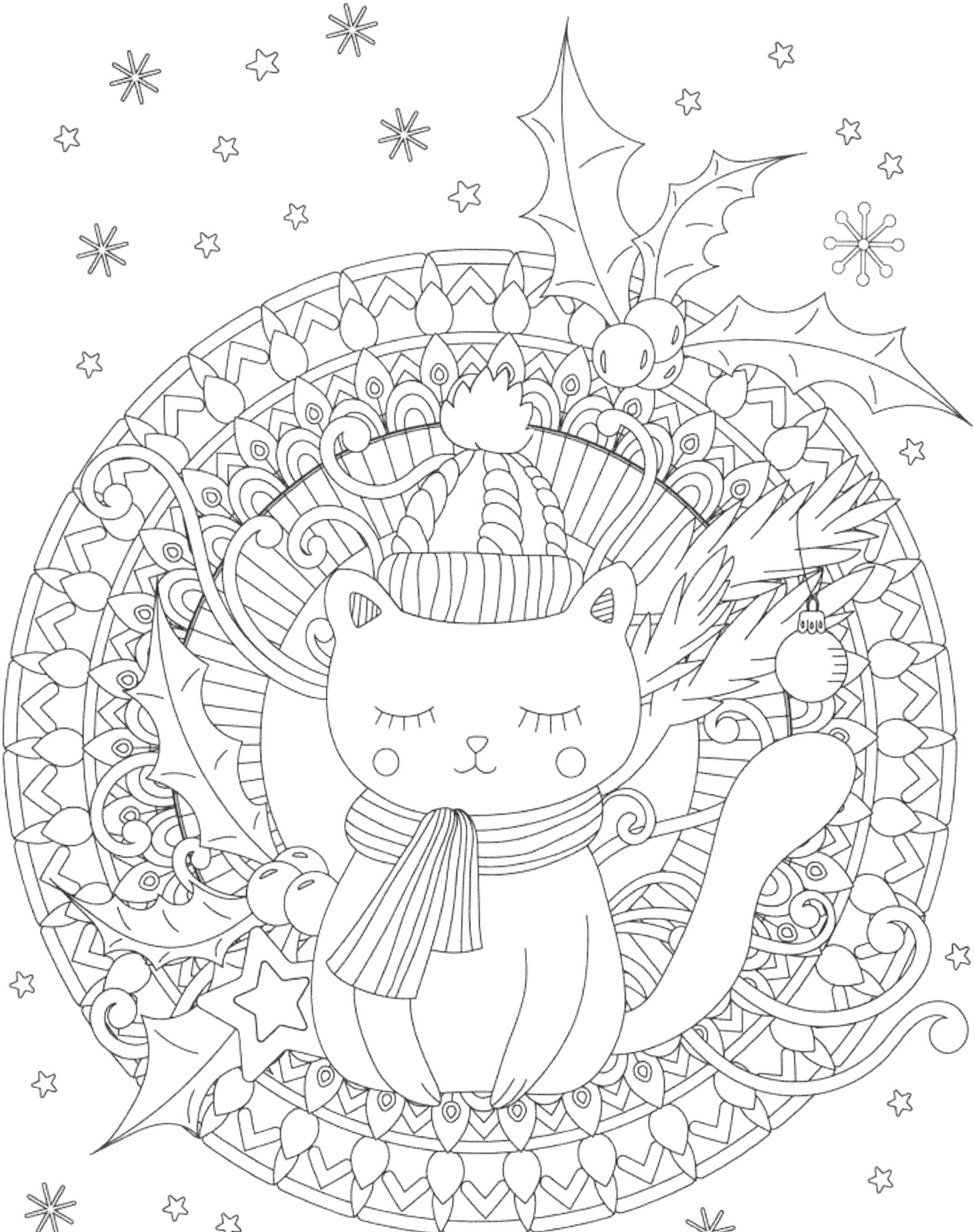

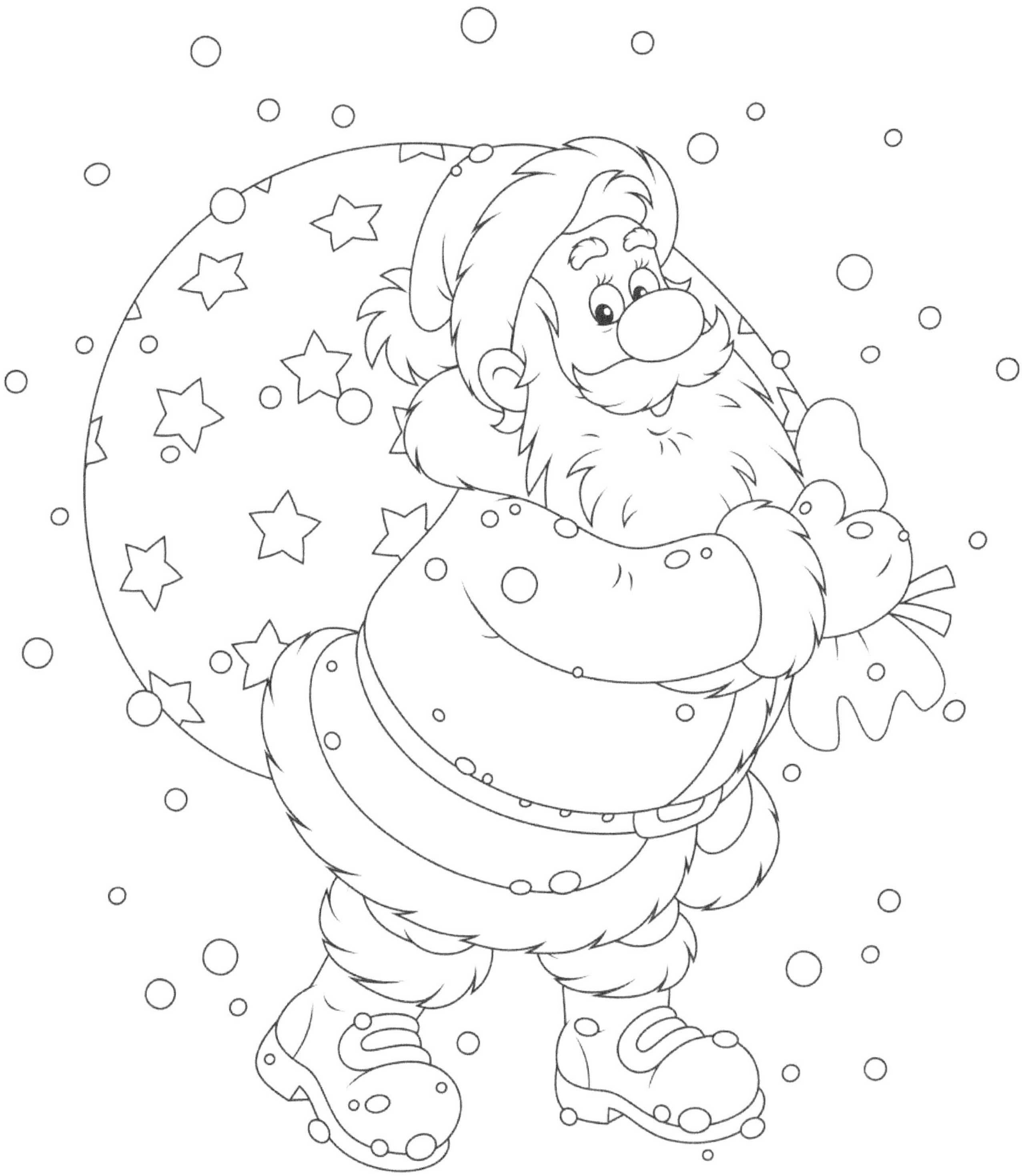

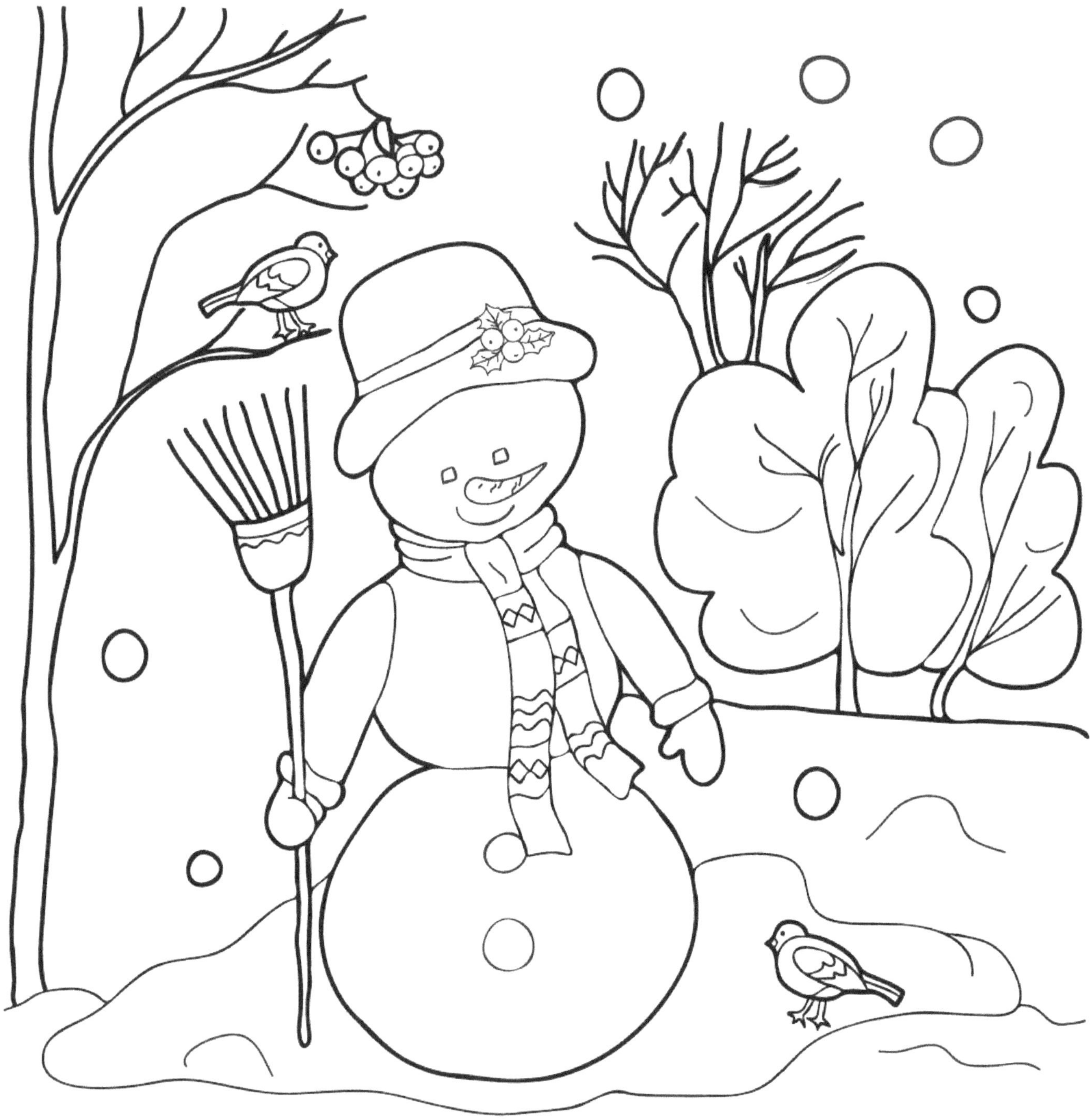

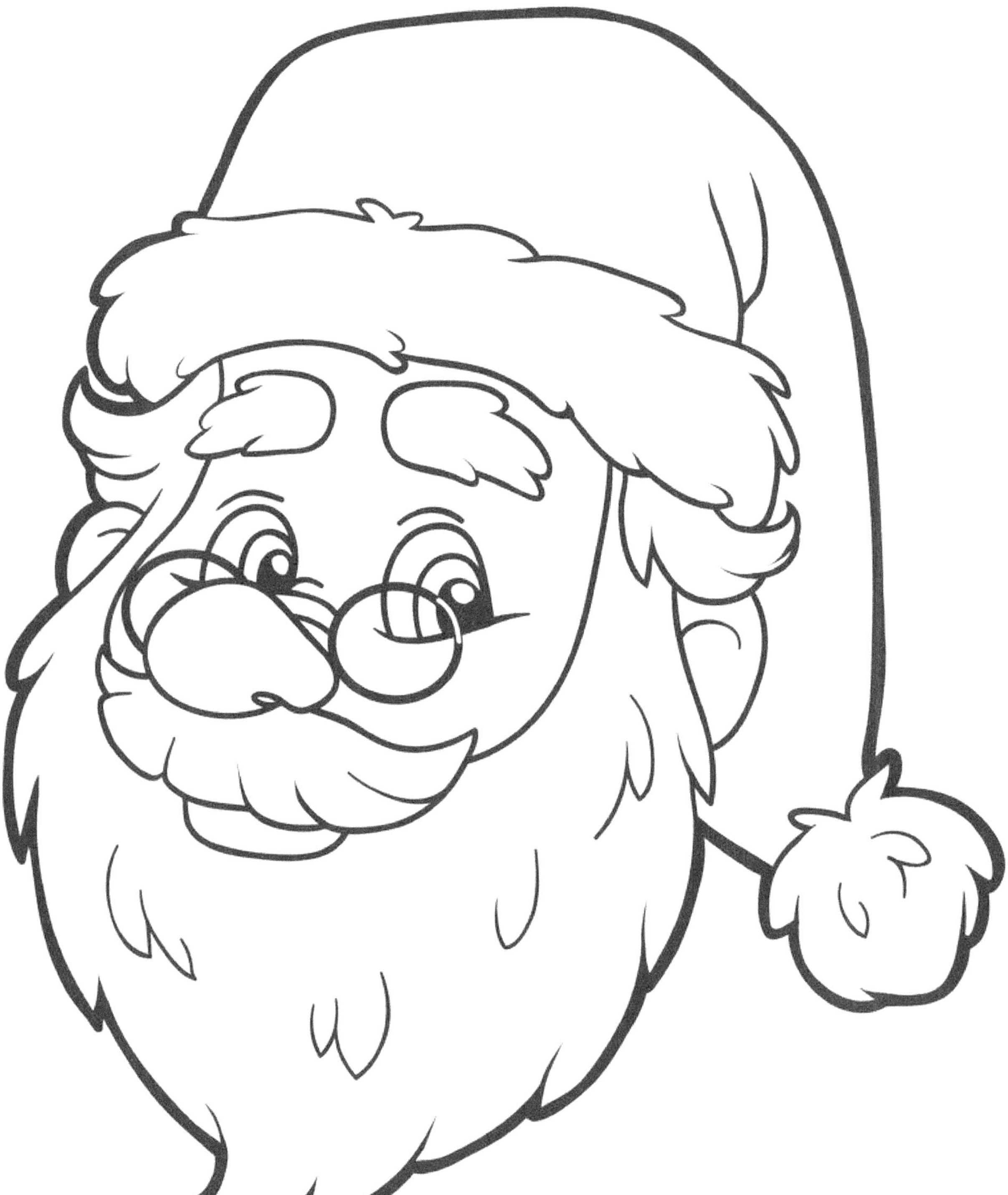

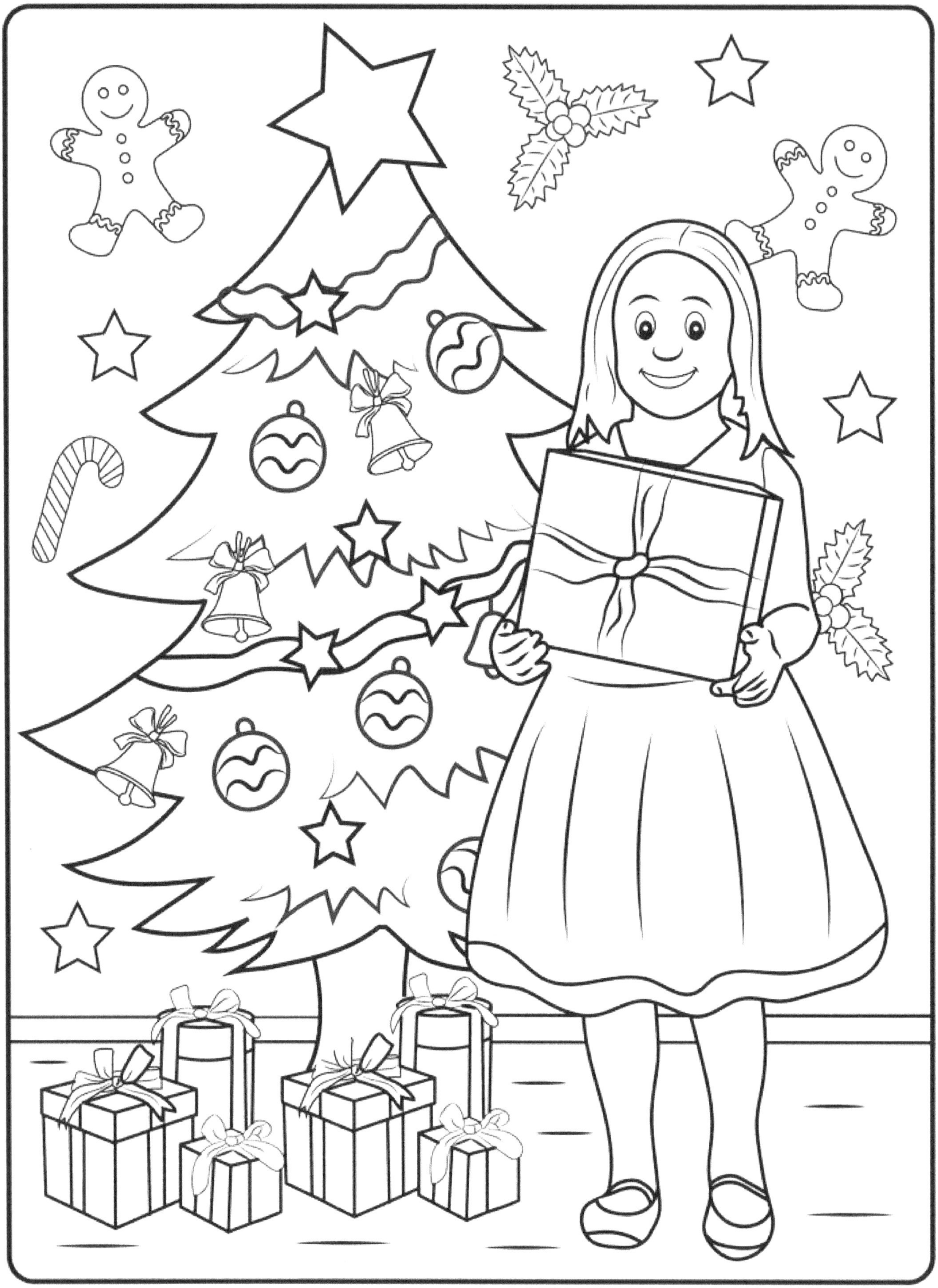

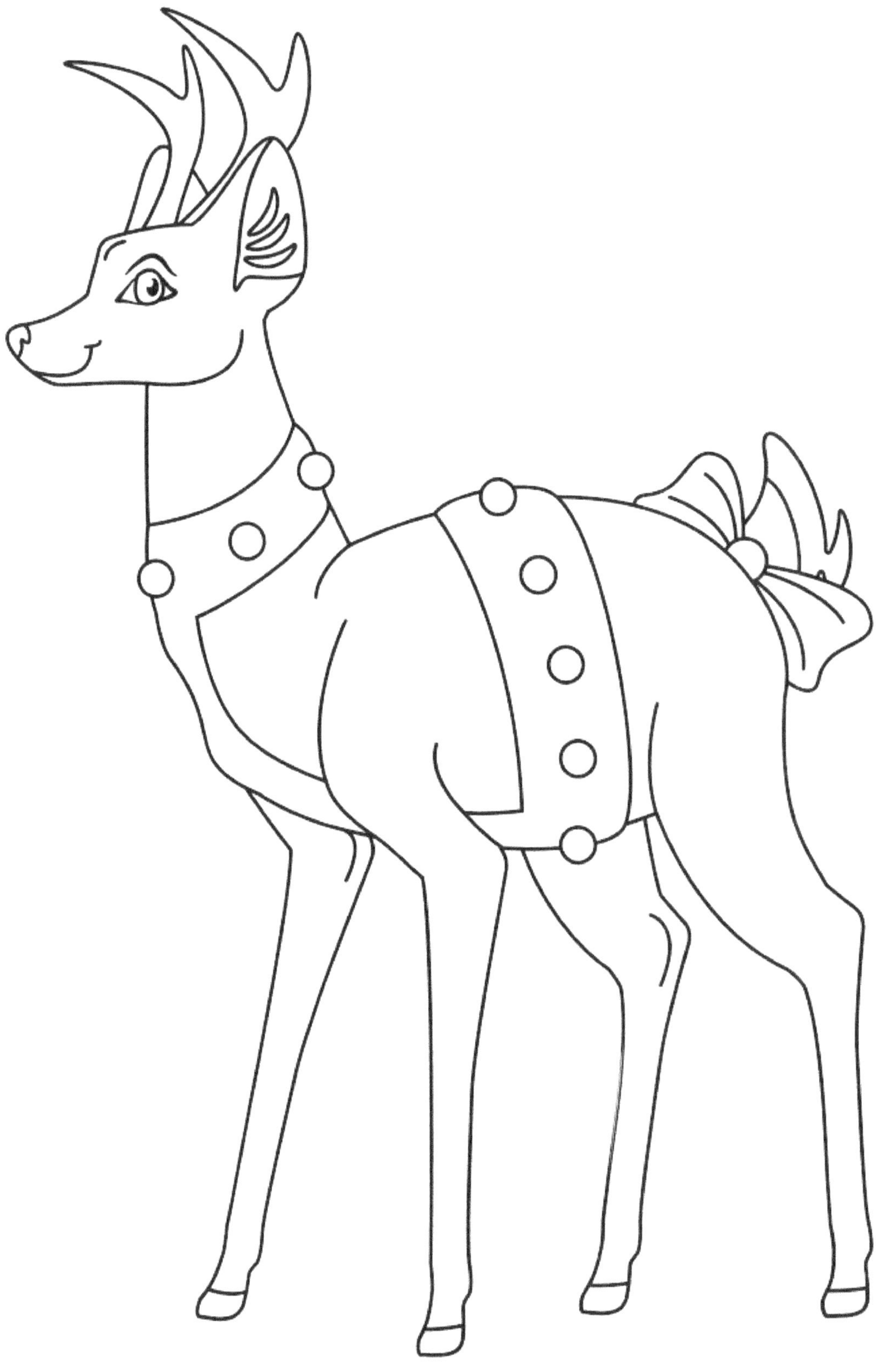

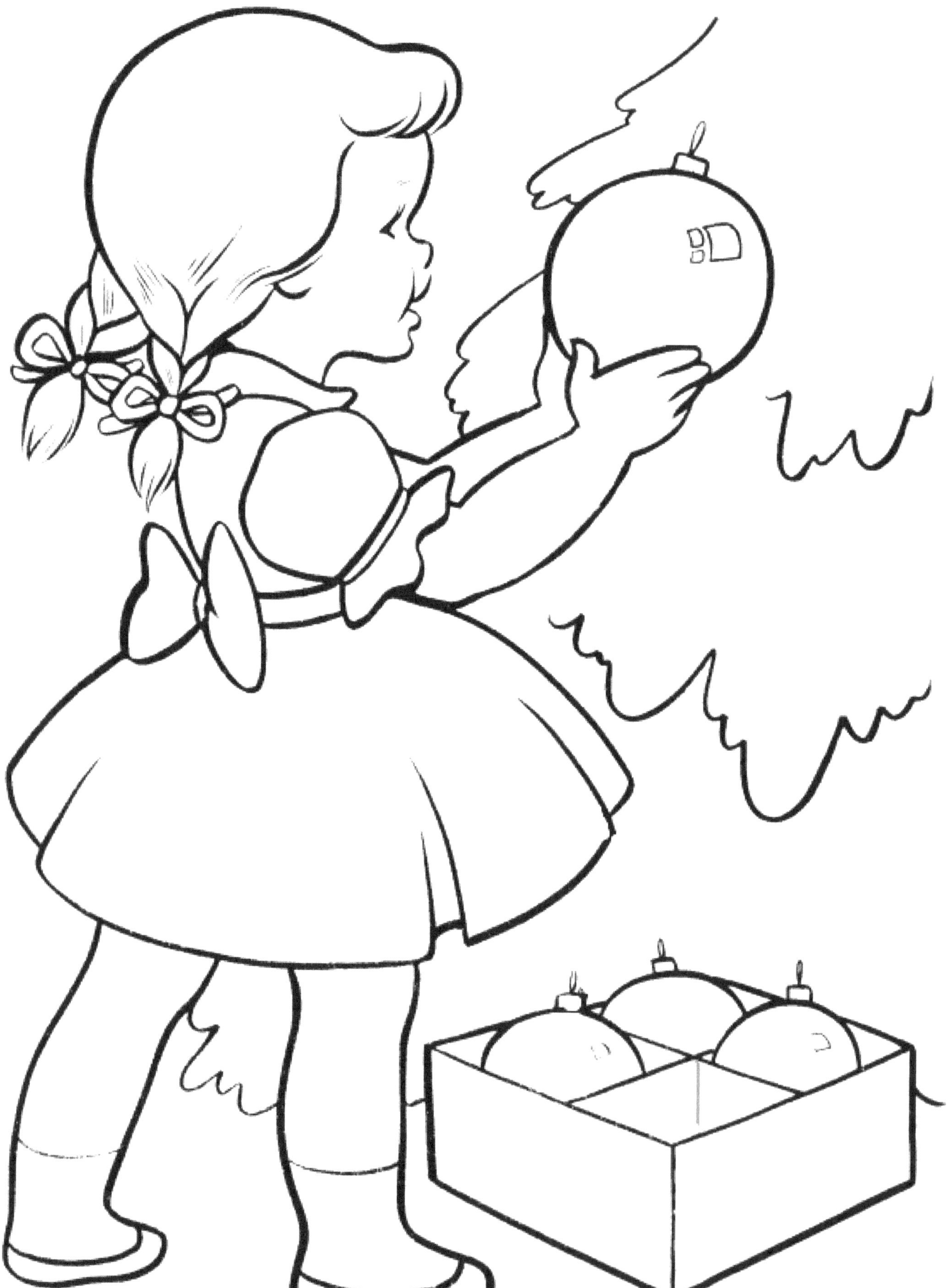

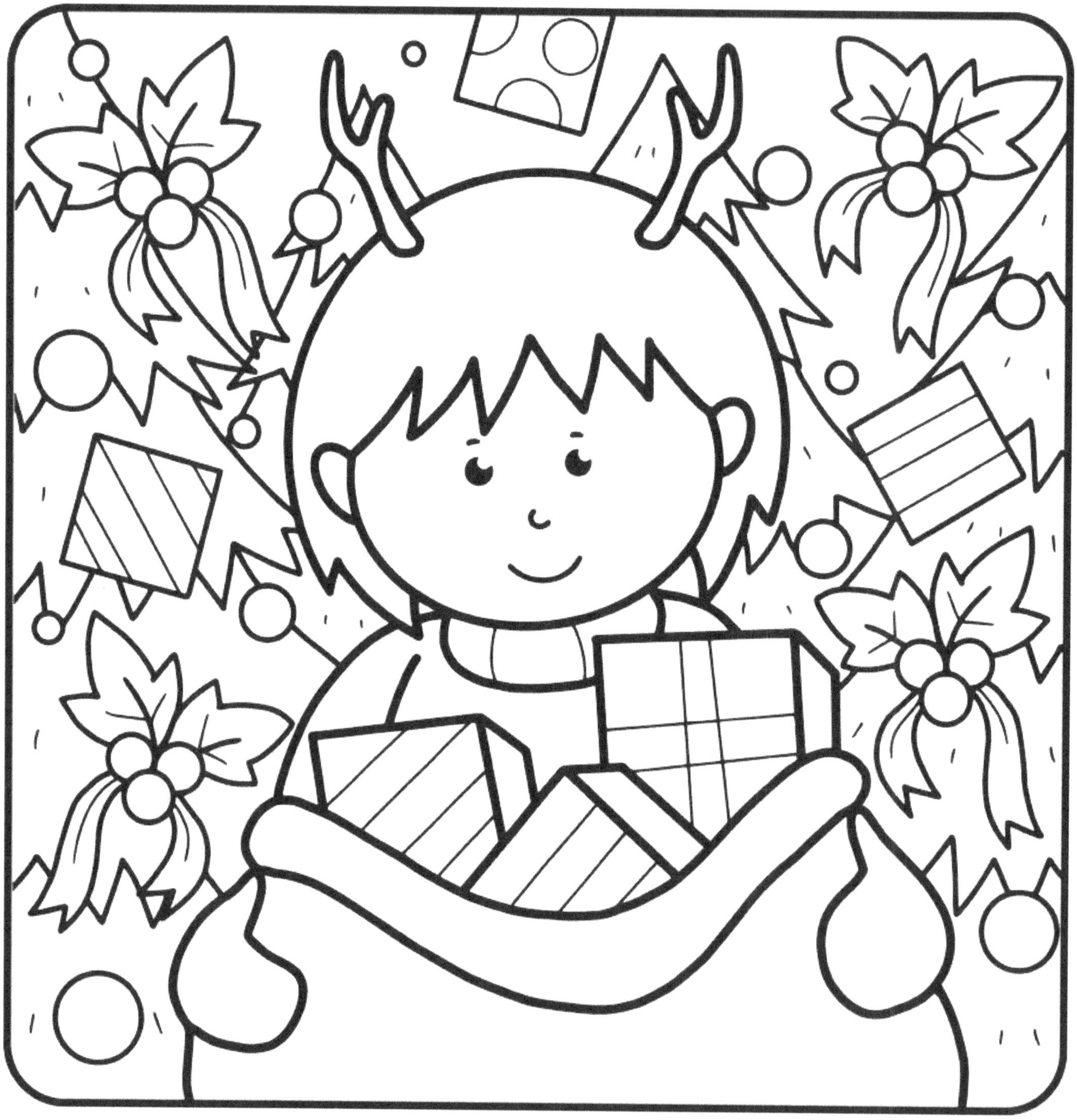

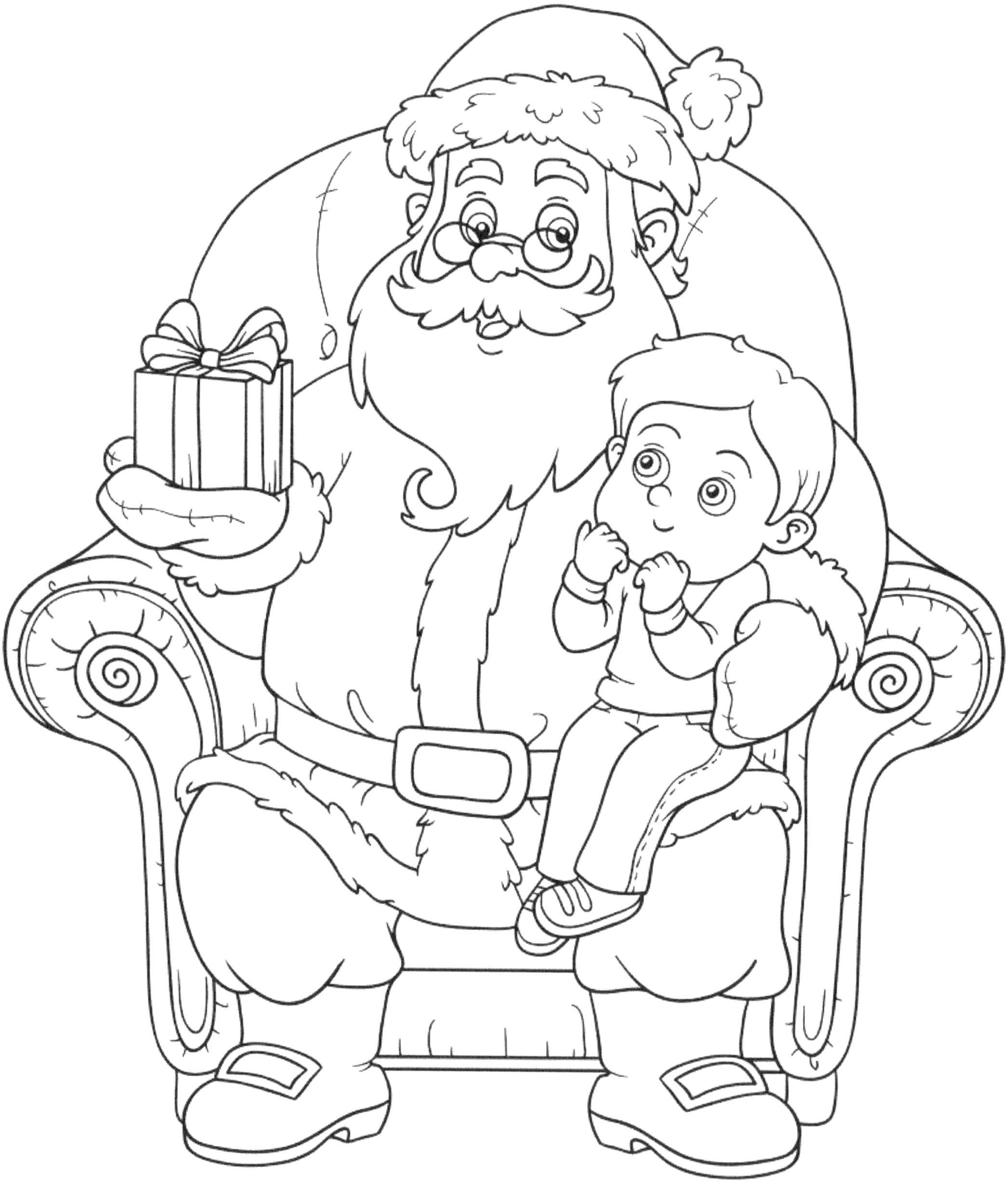

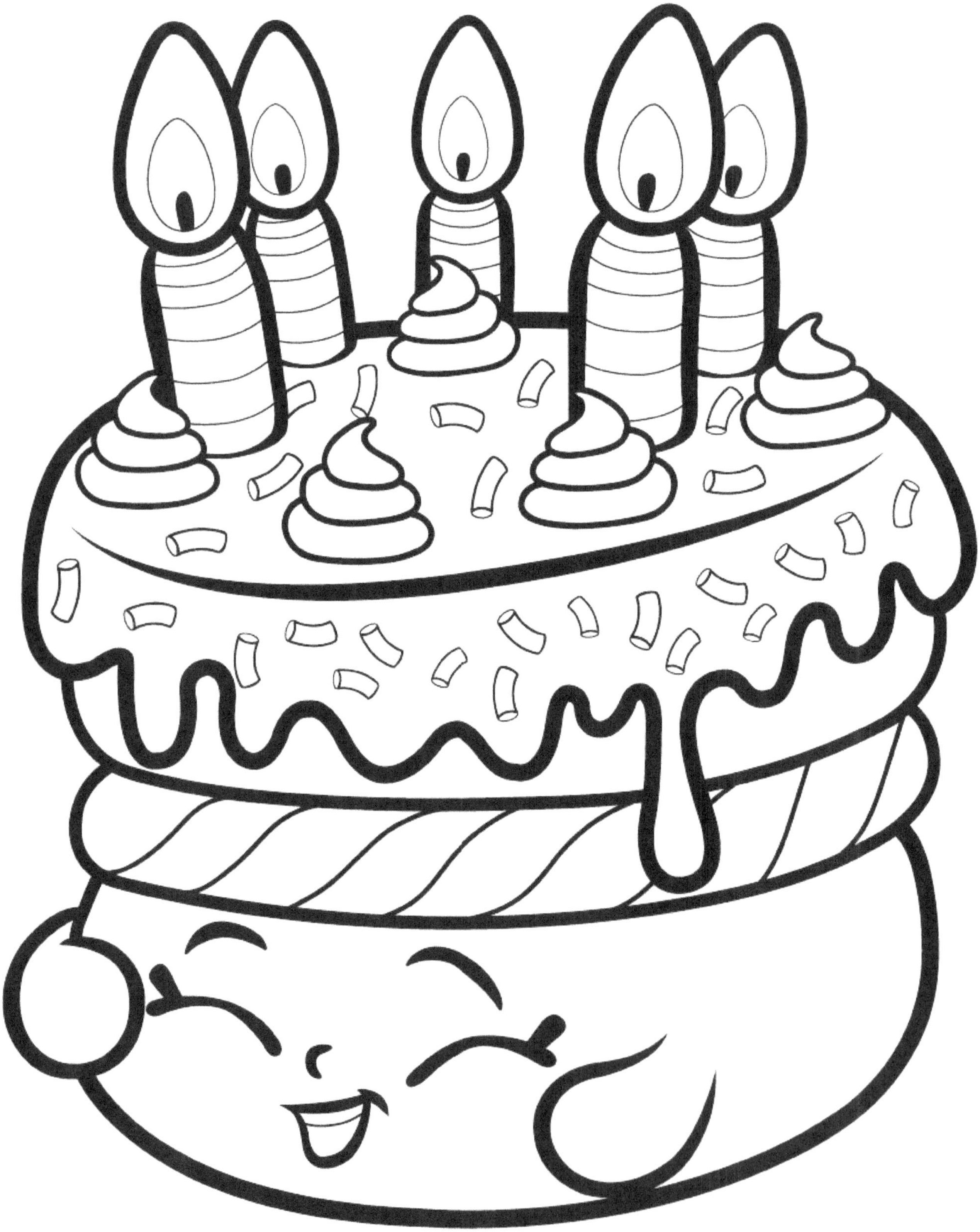

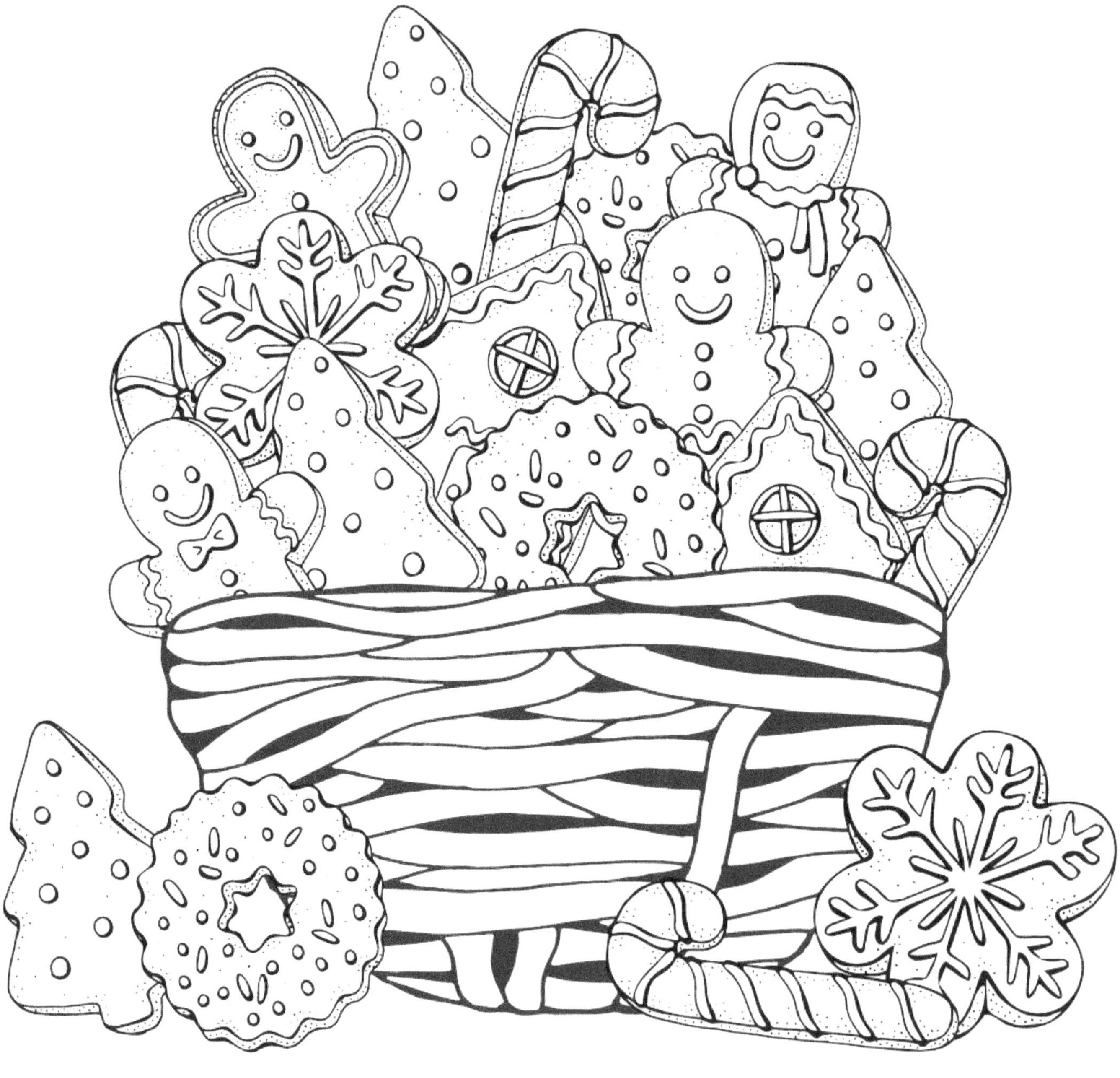

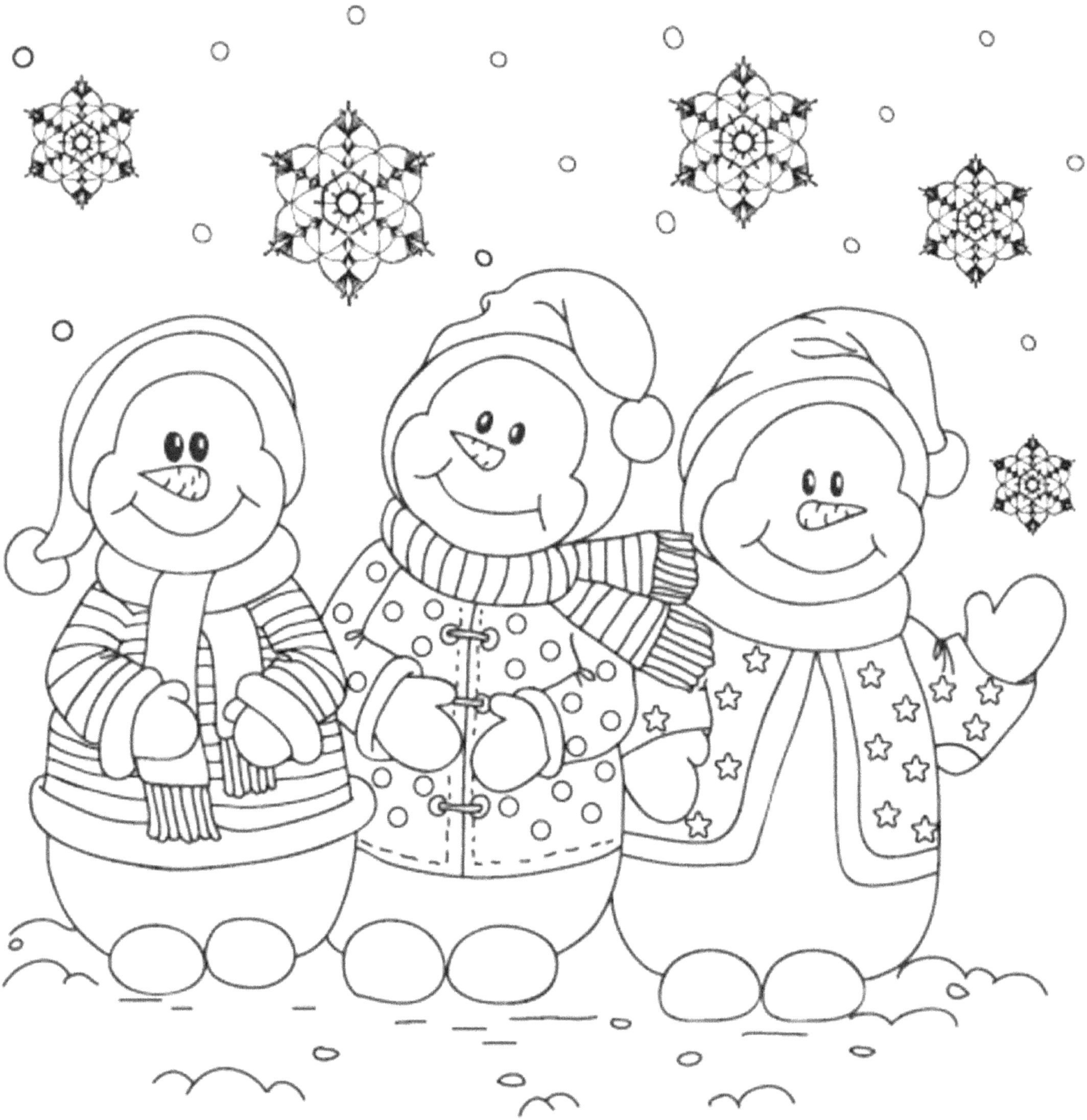

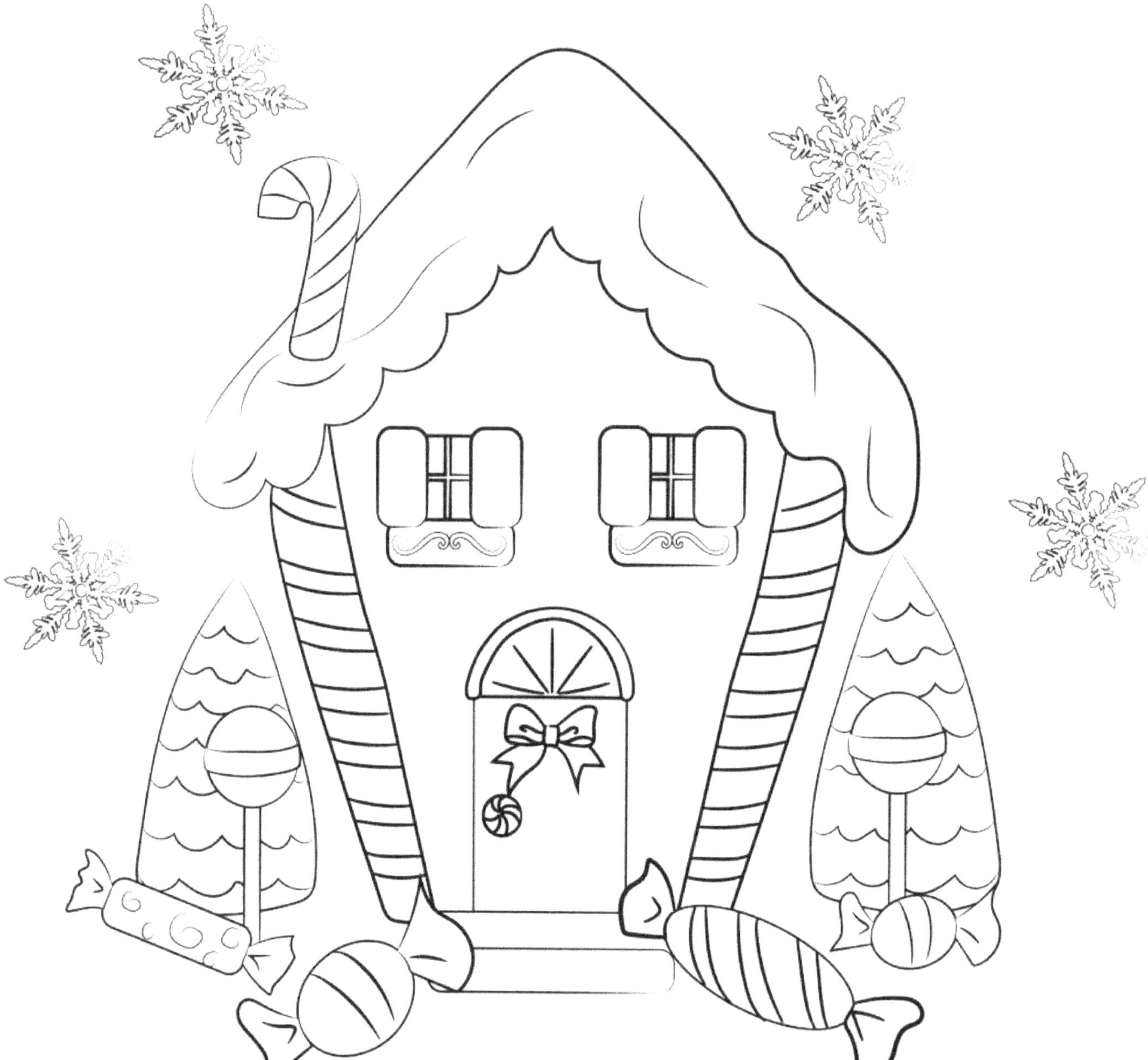

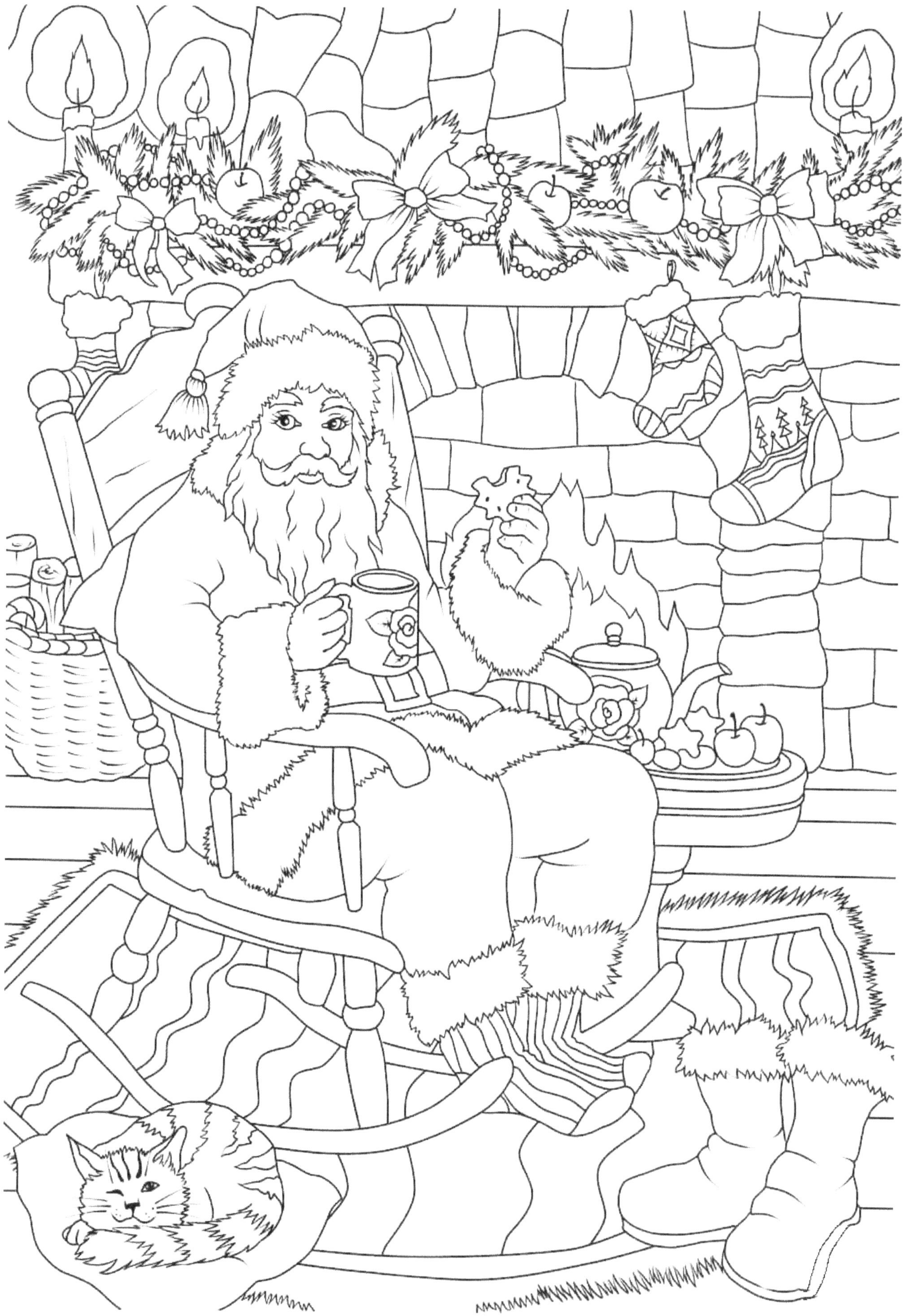

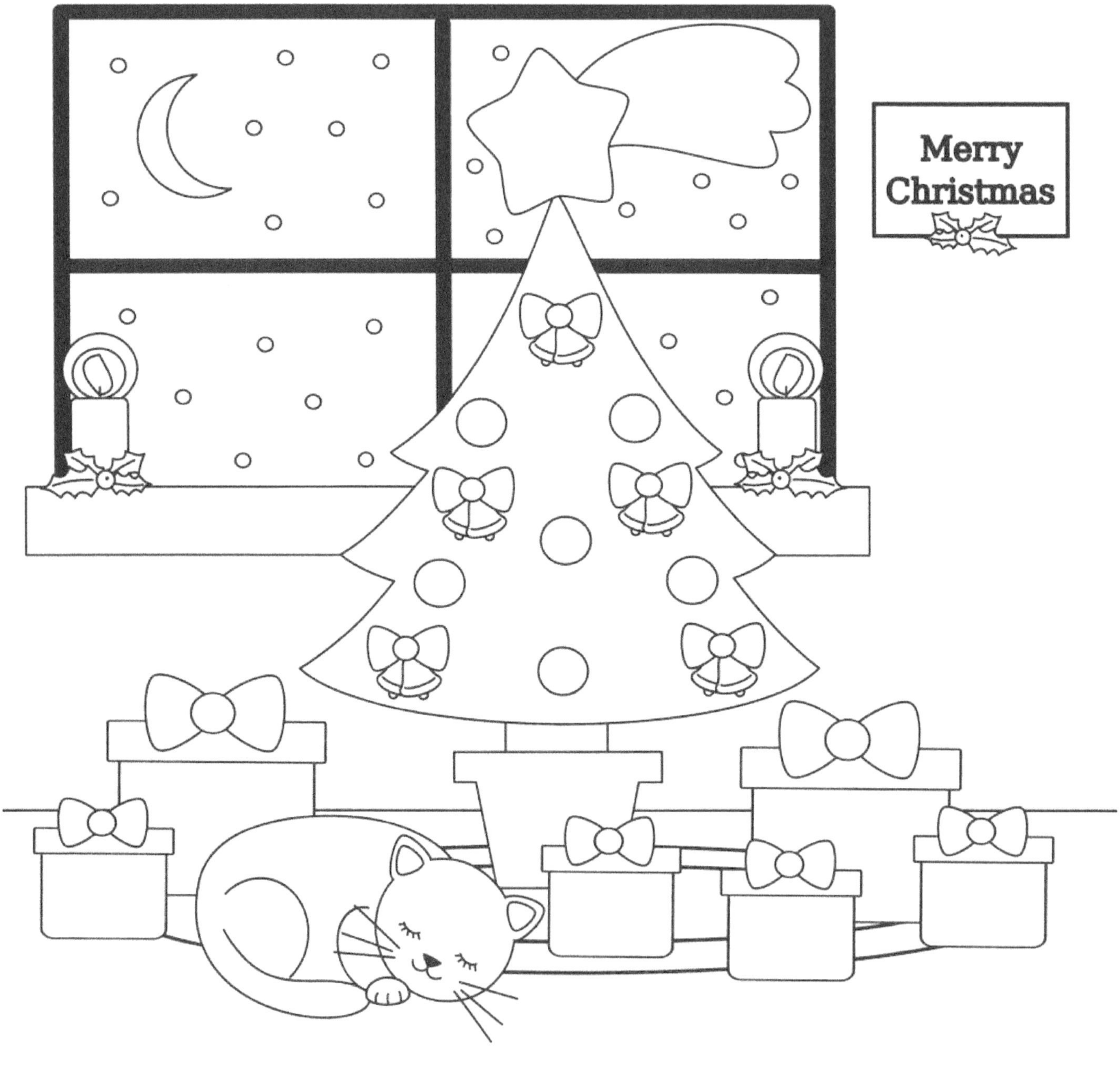
Merry
Christmas

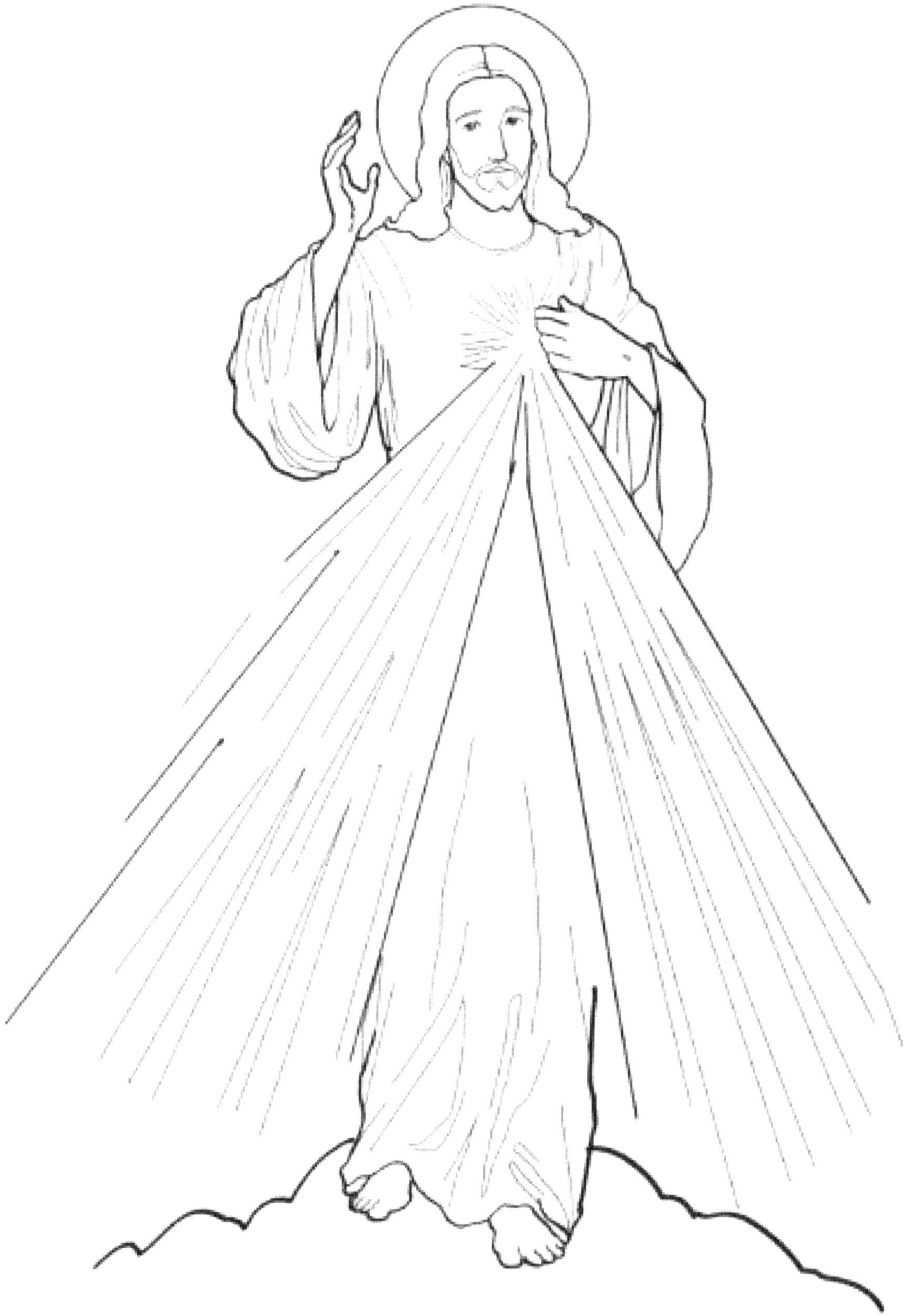

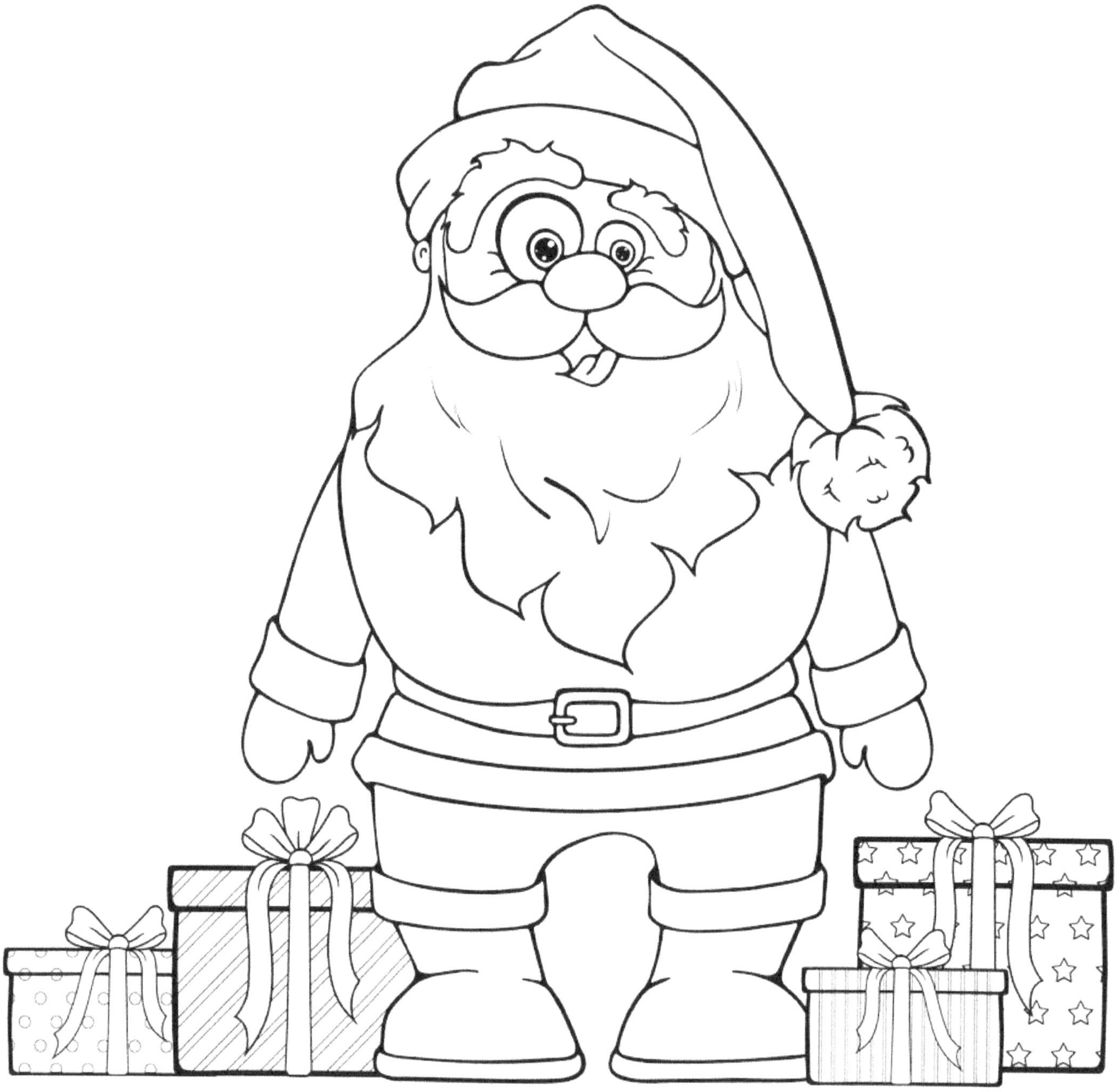

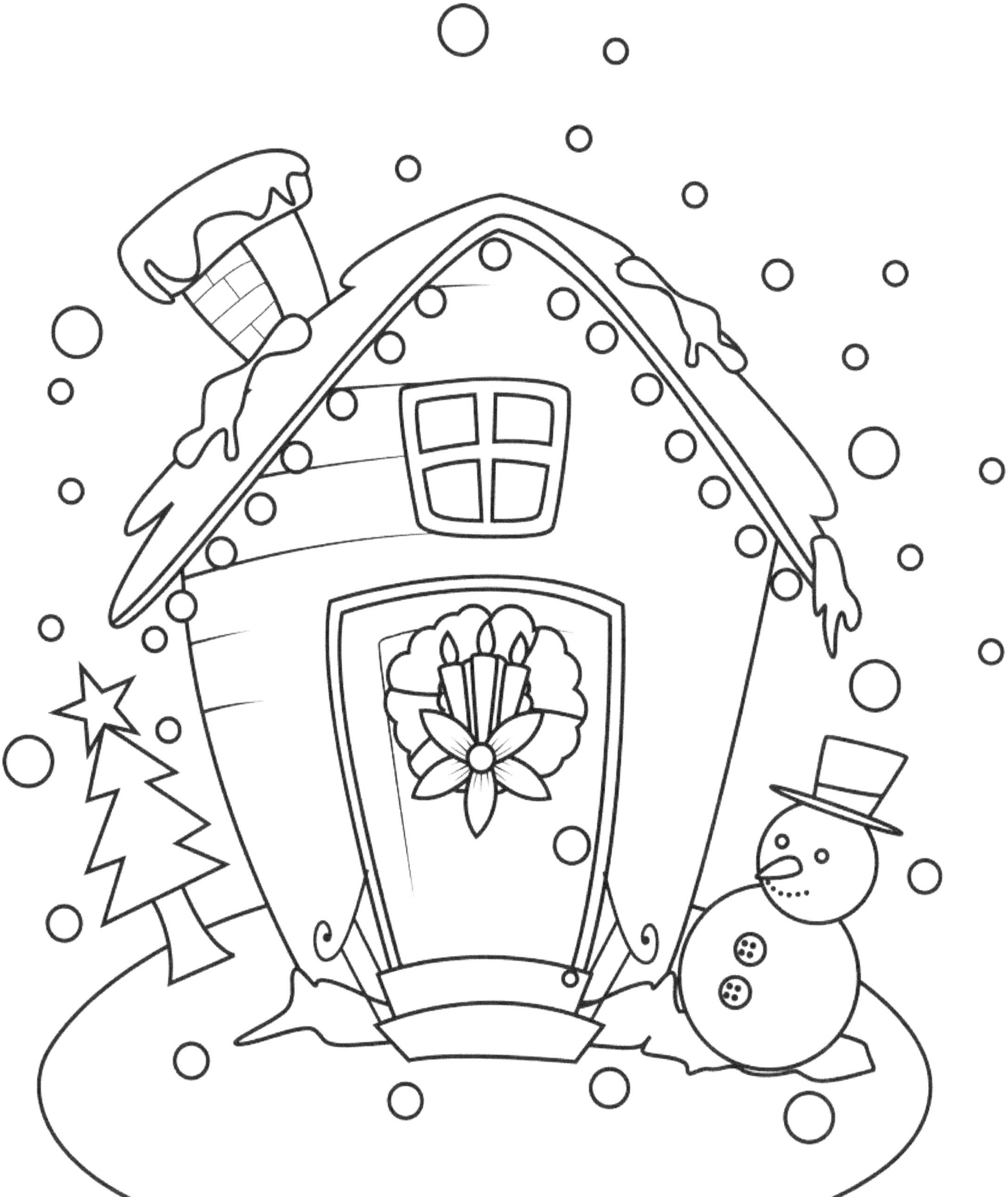

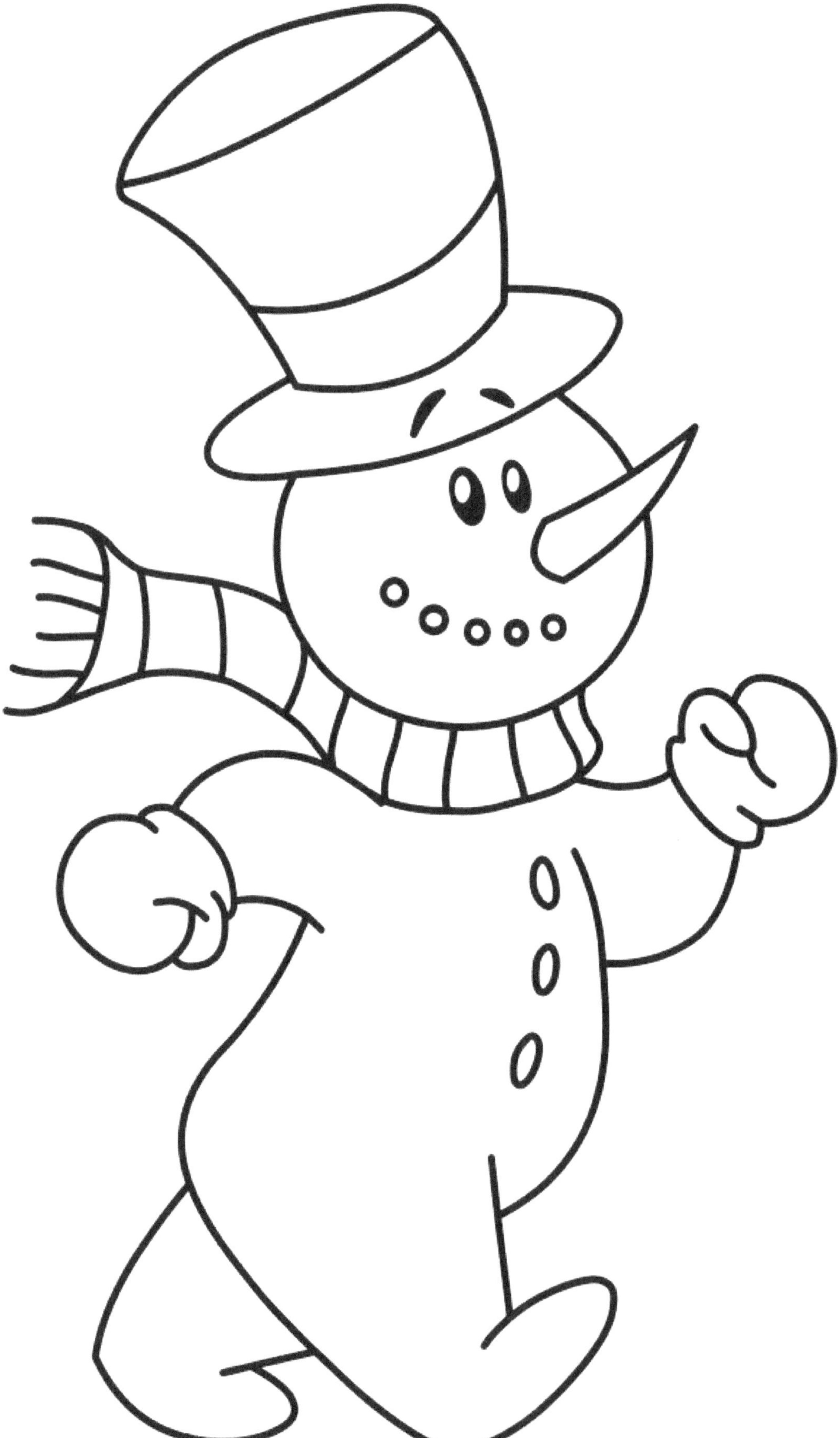

# Write Your Experience

www.ingramcontent.com/pod-product-compliance
Lightning Source LLC
Chambersburg PA
CBHW081731250726
48657CB00010B/3221
* 9 7 9 8 5 7 4 2 5 5 5 9 9 *